❦ *Possibilities*

for Over One Hundredfold
More Spiritual Information

❧ *Possibilities*

for Over One Hundredfold More Spiritual Information

THE HUMBLE APPROACH IN THEOLOGY AND SCIENCE

Sir John Templeton

TEMPLETON FOUNDATION PRESS

PHILADELPHIA AND LONDON

Templeton Foundation Press
Five Radnor Corporate Center, Suite 120
100 Matsonford Road
Radnor, Pennsylvania 19087

Library of Congress Cataloging-in-Publication Data

Templeton, John, 1912–
    Possibilities for over one hundredfold more spiritual information : the humble approach in theology and science / John Marks Templeton.
        p.   cm.
ISBN 1-890151-33-5 (pkb. :alk.paper)
ISBN 1-890151-46-7 (hardcover: alk. paper)
    1. Religion and science. I. Title

BL240.2.T452 2000
200—dc21   00-029917

Printed in Canada

00 01 02 03 04 05 06   10 9 8 7 6 5 4 3 2 1

Contents

Spiritual Information

How little we know—how eager to learn! The "Humble Approach" is an attitude that fosters search and may facilitate the discovery of over 100 fold more spiritual information than humankind has ever possessed before. It welcomes questions and research.

Can worship of our creator focus on awesome mysteries to supplement the old certainties? Can mysteries more readily encourage enthusiasm for progress?

Does increasing evidence indicate that invisible realities may be vastly more basic than things visible? Can research show that the spiritual is the foundation of material life?

Can intellects search for more about basic realities? Can created intellects speed up creativity?

Spiritual information is a realm of study which may expand in ways none can yet predict. But in this book, those words refer to the concepts from religions which have proven beneficial and which need to be supplemented through millions of dollars daily for rigorous verifiable research, especially on those neglected basic invisible realities such as love, purpose, creativity, intellect, thanksgiving, prayer, humility, praise, thrift, compassion, invention, truthfulness, giving and worship.

Already, some thinkers are pondering the concept that every discovery in any science helps humans to enlarge their definition of the word god. For example, can humans learn something about god from x-ray astronomy, by subatomic physics or by quantum nonlocality? Or if the expensive search for extraterrestrial intelligence, SETI, ever succeeds, will we enlarge our theology? If discoveries keep pointing our search toward multiplying mysteries, will we begin to comprehend more about creativity? Clarifying the words *spiritual information* is equally difficult now as the difficulty as recently as 1800 in foreseeing the expansion of medical information or electromagnetic information.

Examples of fruitful spiritual information may result when rigorous researches are applied to some of the ninety-two questions listed in Appendix 1 of this book. If researchers can help spiritual information growth to average 5% yearly, then we can have over 100 fold increase in a single century. Amazingly, experts say that total world information has begun to grow about 25% yearly. Largely this comes from science research supported by about a billion dollars daily.

❦ *Possibilities*

for Over One Hundredfold
More Spiritual Information

CHAPTER ONE

An Introduction for Humble Researchers

1. The focus of this book is to encourage researches for vastly more spiritual information to supplement the wonderful ancient scriptures. (Refer to discussion in book Preface.)

2. We stand on the shore facing a vast, uncertain ocean of reality from which future knowledge will be obtained. How large is this ocean? How far might its exploration take those who will live in the future and for whom what we know now may seem quaint? Clearly it is a vista that should humble us, in a similar way as it did even for the great scientist Sir Isaac Newton. Near the end of his remarkable life (1642–1727) of extraordinary scientific accomplishment, he wrote that to himself he had seemed only "like a boy, playing on the sea-shore, and diverting myself, in now and then finding a smoother pebble or a prettier shell than ordinary, whilst the great ocean of truth lay all undiscovered before me."

3. Indeed Newton was correct scientifically. In 2000 his insights can be mastered by high-school students and college freshman. Physics at the cutting edge has come a long way from his day into our contemporary age of curved space-time, supernova explosion codes, high temperature superconductivity, quantum computation, and ten-dimensional superstrings. There are of course reasons to take great pride in what humanity has learned. But we have also learned that human

knowledge expands and accelerates. So what the future is likely to bring over time surely will make even the most knowledgeable among us seem to be quite limited in our perspectives.

4. We stand upon an impressive bedrock of research and evidence and concepts secured over the latest five centuries of accelerated scientific progress. This vantage point seems secure and impressive. It looms like a high shore cliff. Human accomplishment has thrust high the solid and impressive tectonics of this landscape. But for each increment of altitude gained, the corresponding vista of the unknown sea expands as well. We can see with our creative imaginations only fleeting glimpses of the future visible ahead, flickering in the depths of our own uncharted human ignorance. To a large extent, the future lies before us like an ocean of unexplored reality.

5. It is exciting to be alive and to think about all the wonders of discovery that lie ahead for future generations. Where will it go? What will be its benefits? All we know is that if we knew we would be very surprised, because reality is surprising. The adventure of science has shown us that it is very deep, very subtle, often strange and ever stretching our imaginations and expanding our horizons. Persons who see the world theistically often think how inappropriate it is to imagine, as we sometimes are tempted to do, that divinity who created and sustains a vast evolving universe through eons of cosmic time placed our generation as the completed purpose of a creative process. Maybe we can expand our horizons and invigorate our sense of purpose if we think that god might have placed us at a new beginning. Are we here for the future and to participate in a grand adventure of the spirit?

6. The universe is vast and possibly eternal, whereas we are small and mortal. Yet, how exciting if our creativity were part of a marvelous, as yet uncomprehended plan. Pascal wrote that "it is not from space that I must seek my dignity, but from the government of my thought.

I shall have no more if I possess worlds. By space the universe encompasses and swallows me up like an atom; by thought I comprehend the world." So though we seem insignificant, perhaps our role might be crucial. As human beings we are endowed with mind and spirit and purpose. We can think, imagine and dream. Can we search for future concepts in a rich expanding diversity of human thought? We seem to be permitted in some ways to be created by infinite divinity for an accelerating adventure of creativity.

7. Is there, however, a stumbling block called egotism? Any common closed-minded attitude of humans tempts people to think they might know it all. Egotism as used here refers not so much to the personal flaw but rather to a habit of mind which inhibits the learning process necessary for future progress. As part of a historical legacy of the scientific method, most scientists have learned to avoid the stagnation that comes from accepting a fixed perspective. As a community of inquiry focused on the process of research, they have learned to become epistemologically open-minded, always seeking to discover new insights and new perspectives. They research the wonders of the universe and research many questions which describe what they do not know. When their concepts break down, they devise new hypotheses and test them. They challenge old assumptions, competing with each other in creative professional rivalry. The material progress of human civilization is, in significant degree, in their creative professional hands, guided by open minds eager to explore new areas of information and understanding.

8. Does this appear equally true concerning humanity's spiritual future? Often theologians, religious leaders and laypeople can be blind to obstacles they themselves erect. Many religious people are not yet inspired to hope that the spiritual future could, or should, be improved from anything that has ever been learned before. Many do not imagine that progress in religion may be possible, perhaps by appreciating ways

that sciences have learned to flourish and by being creatively open to a discovery-seeking and future-oriented perspective. For so many religious people, the future of religions seems nothing much beyond the preservation of ancient traditions. Some therefore may not want to consider the possibility of a future of progressively unfolding spiritual discoveries. Yet, if our creativity has significance, then what Newton called the "ocean of truth" may hold wonderful possibilities for the future of religion, as it clearly does for the future of science. Could it be possible that the adventure of science can both inspire and assist religion to explore a rich future of "boundless possibilities"?

9. When human beings take a more humble approach, they can welcome new ideas about the spirit just as they welcome new scientific and technological ideas about how to cure infections, how to heat or cool their homes or how to communicate quickly with people who are far away from them.

10. The humble approach is meant to help as a corrective to parochialism in religion. Humility reminds us that our concepts of god, the universe, even our own selves, may be too limited. It is universally a wise teaching in most of the great religions that we are all too self-centered. We overestimate the small amount of knowledge we possess. To be humble then means to admit the infinity of creation and the boundless possibilities within it. Thus can we become motivated and enthusiastic to search for opportunities for us to engage in creativity and gain benefits from experiences and possibilities we may never have dreamed of before? Such an approach asks each of us, whether we are scientists or mainly active in religious-focused lives, to become open to the possible abundance of spiritual potential in our own lives.

11. The key needed may be to cultivate a spirit of humility simply by being open to the possibility of our existence within a divine reality which dwarfs our personal reality. This spirit of humility can exalt us

with something far greater and with concepts we may hardly have begun to understand. Can we use our talents to explore the universe to discover future concepts? Many evidences indicate that we have been given talents and intelligence with which to participate in this accelerating creative process.

12. Until the emergence of human beings on the face of the earth, evolution proceeded gradually, unfolding the rich complexity of mineral, vegetable and animal life. Now with human intelligence capable of studying the creator and his creation, evolution need no longer travel only on its previous slow path. Possibly it was the creator's plan that one day his children could serve as useful tools for his creative purposes.

13. At this present moment, the human race, even after thousands of years of historical development, is still at the dawn of new creation. This is a tremendous, awe-inspiring responsibility. It should humble us.

14. Can humility be a key to our future progress? Without it, will we be too self-satisfied with past glories to launch boldly into the challenges ahead? Without a hunger to explore new possibilities and a restlessness to transcend our ignorance, will we be wide-eyed and open-minded enough to discover new areas for research? If we are not humble enough to learn as children learn, we may be unable to admit mistakes, seek advice and try again. The humble approach creates enthusiasm for all of us who are concerned about improving the future of civilization. It is an inspirational approach for all of us who are not satisfied to let things drift and who want instead to channel our creative restlessness toward helping to build a world in which progress is vigorous in spiritual aspects of life as well as in scientific, technological and economic ones.

15. Every person's concept of god is too small. Through humility might we begin to glimpse encouraging glimmerings of the infinity of god? Could we develop a hunger to explore boundless new possibilities? This is the spirit of the humble approach.

16. It is also in open-minded humility that we can learn from each other. An attitude of humility can allow us to be open to each other and ready to see things from another's point of view and share ours with others freely. Through humility we can avoid the sins of pride and intolerance and avoid especially harmful religious strife because it is unlikely any religion could know more than a tiny bit about an infinite god. Humility opens the door to being hungry to discover basic realities of the spirit. Especially, it may allow us to discover ways to learn more, possibly by research methods and perhaps thereby to accelerate progress within religions in the future.

17. Twenty-five centuries ago Xenophanes and twelve centuries ago Shankara taught that maybe nothing exists independently of god and that god is immeasurably greater than all time and space, let alone the visible earth. But only in the 20th century have modern sciences come to realize how very tiny the earth is compared with the billions of galaxies and how very brief human history is in comparison with the age of the cosmos. Contemporary physics is beginning to unveil hitherto undreamed of aspects and even possibly new dimensions of reality that constitute a mysterious and wondrously rich and complex invisible space-time that generates and holds together within its astonishing configuration all that humans can directly observe. The nature of the cosmos hinted at by the direction of fundamental research indicates intricate, complex and sometimes bizarre realities reaching out beyond the known, inspiring wonder and inviting further inquiry. Can humility open the way forward toward even more astonishing aspects of reality?

18. It is hoped that this book will reach many people who have an interest in exploring the possibility that research methods can generate spiritual progress. Can our minds be stretched far beyond the range of their grasp hitherto?

19. Perhaps people will be uplifted and inspired to catch glimpses of unexpected aspects of reality that beckon their inquiry. It is clear that this is a radical notion. Yet, perhaps learning if it is possible to advance research into spiritual reality can be a fruitful exploratory effort, simply to see if there are ways to move forward beyond limits we might ordinarily expect. Were such a goal possible, how fruitful it might be to pursue it. But if we do not even think to try, then how will we know what we will have missed? But if we discovered or had some inkling, then we might be eager to devote our time, talents, creativity and financial resources toward promoting spiritual research.

20. Many highly educated people feel that religion is obsolete. In some senses they may have a point. We typically do not observe the kind of dynamism in religion that we see in other areas of life such as science, technology and business. To many, religion sometimes seems like a kind of history museum which lacks the excitement and vibrancy of other aspects of life that constantly experience innovation.

21. Could young people and intellectuals be attracted to forms of religion that are genuinely dynamic and rapidly progressing? Does this mean that the old ways have to be discarded totally? I hope not, because it is clear that much of the strength of religion is in the precious core of wisdom and truth that it transmits from each generation to the next. So opening up a few religious communities to new concepts and new adventures of spiritual learning should not be like a revolution which attempts to build the new upon the ashes of the old. My own hopes for rescuing various religions from obsolescence would be for the visions and the teachings of the great prophets and teachers of the past not to be disputed. Rather they should be studied again and considered together with recent concepts of reality as springboards toward creating new and even expanded understanding of divinity and inspiration in worship and ritual.

22. This book begins to explore the possibility that developing a humble approach in theology, which encourages research and engages carefully with science, may be even more fruitful than endeavors to reinvigorate inherited systems of thought, whether they be polytheistic, deistic, theistic, monotheistic, pantheistic, panentheistic or even older concepts. Gradually each of us may learn to feel unlimited love for every person, with never any exception, and be grateful for an increasingly rich diversity of thought emanating from research and worship in every land. One of the purposes of this book is to examine or foster the idea that through an expanded search for more knowledge, in which we are open-minded and willing to experiment, theology may produce positive results even more amazing than the discoveries of scientists that have electrified the world with their discoveries in the 20th century.

23. Some experts rather roughly estimate that the total of practically useful information available to human beings has increased over a million fold since Gutenberg invented movable type, a period that is only 10% of the age of human religions, which in turn is less than one millionth of our sun's history. Total information is likely to increase over another millionfold just in the 21st century. But how long will we humans take to multiply even 100 fold our spiritual information? (Refer to discussion in book Preface.)

24. Why do so many intelligent people think theology may have become obsolete, that it no longer addresses reality? Surely, few intelligent people think of physics or astronomy as obsolescent? That is the subject of this book, *Possibilities for Over One Hundredfold More Spiritual Information: The Humble Approach in Theology and Science*. Theology was once considered as queen of the sciences. It may someday regain that title; but first we may have to learn how to learn in order to regain that title. The Templeton Foundations are eager to make initial investments in careful and rigorous research in order to

seek new possibilities. Initially, we realize that it is important to move forward in a clear and rigorous manner and to research topics which may seem quite simple, as, for example, how participating in religious life can help you to be healthier, or how the human mind has an intrinsic spiritual perspective or how the laws of physics seem conspiratorially arranged to allow consciousness or creativity. Later, if some of these studies are successful and are persuasive to skeptics, then we may see more and more research opportunities. Part of science itself and of the humble approach is working on simple, tractable problems and refining the researcher's methods and hypotheses.

25. A major aim of the Templeton Foundations is to help those relatively rare and visionary entrepreneurs who are trying to encourage all religions to become enthusiastic about the concepts of spiritual progress and new spiritual information, especially by linking with scientific methods and lines of inquiry. If benefits from this approach can be practically demonstrated, then it may be welcomed and can help to reinvigorate appreciation for and to supplement the wonderful ancient scriptures which stand at the core of most religious cultures. The words "new additional spiritual information, especially through science research, to supplement the wonderful ancient scriptures" refers to the probability that vastly expanded research, including research methods and instruments beyond present human concepts, can expand human concepts of divinity and of accelerating creativity (and human help in creativity) and can find various ways to measure or test basic forces and realities (presently beyond sight and touch). There may be significant promise in supporting a wide range of careful and rigorous research projects by well-regarded scientists on basic areas with theological relevance and potential, such as love, prayer, purpose, altruism, creativity, thanksgiving and worship.

26. By reading and writing in this field, scientists and other laypersons may not only enhance their own spiritual growth but also stimu-

late progress and expand the whole field of theology in ways that may benefit all. Maybe in small ways a spiritual and religious renaissance may have started already that can grow and flourish over time.

27. Is evidence increasing that human concepts have always been and are now too tiny? May reality be over 100 fold more vast and complex than concepts by animals or humans? Do history and geology indicate that people who thought they already had the total truth, whether three thousand years ago or now, can become obsolete? As one example, the great reptiles that ruled our little planet vastly longer than humans have yet ruled could have been so egotistic as to conceive of god as a wise dinosaur. Possibly present human concepts may be pitiful also.

28. Is it possible we live in a universe full of life distributed over hundreds of billions of different worlds? Could beings exist vastly more wise and sophisticated than we? Would they have concepts of divinity and practices that could be called religion, possibly vastly deeper and more sublime than we can even imagine? Is reality vastly greater than things visible or tangible to humans? Is love more universal than the universe? Could it be true that in a deep way, a purpose toward love really may govern the sun and stars? The humble approach is about many questions. How little we know—how eager to learn! This is the humble approach.

29. As mentioned above, experts studying the recent expansion of information estimate that total information now doubles each three years. This means than in only thirty years information may be one thousandfold more, and in only sixty years humans may possess a million times as much information. Then maybe it is modest to hope that ways can be found for over 100 fold more spiritual information in the 21st century. The benefits from over 100 fold more spiritual information might exceed the benefits now so obvious from over 100 fold more information in the sciences achieved in the 20th century.

CHAPTER TWO

Humble
About What?

1. The word *humility* has a range of meanings and easily can be misunderstood in the present context. In common usage it often may describe the virtue of serving others, as, for example, in the famous saying of Jesus that "among you, whoever wants to be great must be your servant, and whoever wants to be first must be willing to be the slave of all" (Matthew 20:26–27 NEB). But, the virtue of humility directed toward humans, however important, is not the focus of this book. The specific perspective focused upon in this book is the humility that humans may need to adopt intellectually and spiritually when hoping to grasp a sense of the enormity of divinity.

2. By the word *humility* we are not referring to self-denigration but instead to recognition that no human has yet found even 1% of those basic invisible realities called spiritual, such as love, purpose, consciousness, intellect, creativity, worship and thanksgiving. This humility creates enthusiasm for diligent research and open-mindedness and free competition in pioneering, as the mysteries of reality unfold with each new discovery. The word *humility* is used in this book to mean admission that god infinitely may exceed anything anyone has ever said of him; and that divinity may be infinitely beyond human comprehension and understanding. A prime purpose of this book is to help us become more humble and thereby reduce the stumbling blocks subconsciously

arising from our own egos. If the word heaven means eternal peace and joy, then can we observe that some persons already have more of it than others? Have you observed that these are generally persons who have reduced their egos, those who desire to give rather than to get? As we grow older and wiser, we often grow in humility.

3. The humble approach may have much in common with but is not the same as natural theology, process theology or empirical theology. Where it may go further is in two basic areas. First, it does not attempt to form a philosophical school. And second, it aims to move forward in a fully exploratory manner principally by sponsoring research projects of a rigorous scientific character and by following up research successes where they are demonstrable. This can be both a difficult and also relatively humble strategy because it does not wish to define a metaphysical roadmap but rather to see how far one can go in exploring the "great ocean of reality" if one tries rather concertedly to follow initial research opportunities in a rigorous scientific mode across a wide range of topics. These may derive from broadly interesting themes— for example, altruistic love—which themes are potentially scientifically tractable in a variety of contexts and also touch on great theological themes, especially ones broadly common to most major traditions. Again, these initially may provide avenues simply for learning how to learn. The humble approach expects that humans can discover and comprehend only a few of the infinite aspects of god's nature, never enough to form a final theology. The humble approach searching for more information about divinity may be a science still in its infancy, but it seeks to develop ways of searching for our creator appropriate to divine infinity and our littleness. The humble approach is a search which looks forward, not backward, and which expects continually to grow from the research of various experts in many methods of inquiry and to learn from its mistakes.

4. It seems plausible that some aspects of nature may reveal some limited attributes of its creator. Humans face limits attempting to learn all about god, the creator, by studying nature. Nature in all its complexity and beauty is only a contingent and partial manifestation of his creativity and power. Hence, as many critics have asserted, natural theology is limited.

5. Recently a new concept of theology may be developing which can be called theology through science. This denotes the way in which scientists are reflecting about the creator at the foundation of their observations of the astronomic and subatomic domains, but also at the foundation of investigations into living organisms and their evolution, and such invisible and complex realities as the human mind, consciousness, purpose and creative intellect.

6. Such experimental theology has revealed so far only a very little about divinity. It begins with a few simple forms of inquiry, subject to little disagreement, and proceeds to probe more deeply in thousands of various ways. Spiritual realities are not easily quantifiable, of course, but there may be aspects of spiritual life which can be demonstrated experimentally one by one, even though there may be hundreds of failures for each success. This approach could be seen as similar to that of experimental medicine. When Thomas A. Edison Laboratories invented the electric light bulb just before the 20th century, they tried one hundred methods before they succeeded.

7. As with experimental theology, the humble approach hopes that there can be a growing body of information and an evolving theology not limited to any one nation or cultural area. Should the truly humble be so open-minded that they welcome spiritual information from any place in the universe that is peopled with intelligent life? Seekers following the humble approach should never be so narrow-minded that they fail to study concepts from other nations, religions or eras.

Because the humble approach to theology is intended to be ongoing and constantly evolving, it may never become obsolete.

8. Perhaps when desiring to learn about divinity, a planetary approach may be much too small. Even a universe-wide approach may be much too small. The picture over 90% of people have of god seems small. Have you heard it said that "god is part of life"? Would it not be wiser to say of humanity that it is only an infinitesimal speck of all that has its being in and through god? Our own egos often tend to make us believe that we are the center of existence. But, could it be more realistic to consider our individual realities as only tiny temporal outward manifestations of a vast universe of being which subsists in the eternal and infinite reality, which some call god? Surely if that is more plausible, then life is a part of god, not vice versa. Or take another example. Have you heard the words "the realm of the Spirit"? Is there any other realm? Humanity on this little earth may be an aspect of unlimited Spirit, rather than belittle the Spirit as an "aspect" of us earthlings. To say that god is a "part" or an "aspect" of life may be as blind as for a person standing on a shore looking at a wave to say, "The ocean is an aspect of that wave."

9. The ocean-wave analogy may be helpful in thinking of divinity with more humility. A wave is part of the ocean, having no existence apart from the larger body of water. The wave is temporary, whereas oceans are relatively permanent. Each wave is different from each other wave. In a sense, the wave is created from the ocean and is a child of the ocean. When it dies, it returns to and continues to be a part of the surging oceans yielding ever new breakers on the beach. Humility seeks to see that a relation may be more productive if viewed in the context of what might be imagined as a possible divine frame of reference, rather than from our own limited perspective. It is such sense of proportion and relationship that those studying the humble approach seek to encourage.

10. The humble approach research respects the hierarchy of being which is evident in creation. Consider a tree. The tree is alive, having been created just as we were. Like us, it consists of billions of cells and atoms. It ages, dies and usually produces seeds after its kind. But the tree cannot describe us. It has no ability to comprehend us or the complex culture of which it is a mere part. It may be a beautiful addition to our garden. We may nourish and care for it. But the difficulty the tree would have in describing us is perhaps similar to our difficulty in writing an account of god. If any person were to say he knew all about god, it might be like a tree claiming to know all about its gardener. Following the humble approach, we can gain some concept of a great ladder of being. Humans may not be the top rung.

11. Perhaps what we know is by analogy as limited as what an ant knows crawling along a shelf in the Library of Congress, or a cricket outside the walls of CERN in Geneva, or a bacterium in the Mayo Clinic, or a fly at the Space Telescope Science Institute, or a worm crawling in a lawn at Cal Tech or Bell Labs or the Institute for Advanced Study at Princeton—or perhaps a butterfly wafting its way beautifully through Silicon Valley.

12. The challenge of these analogies is the *perspective shift*. We have no difficulty understanding that a beetle is an insect and that it has limited perception. Neither do we have difficulty understanding that vast knowledge resides in Massachusetts Institute of Technology due to the brilliant humans who work there. It is far more difficult for us to think that our perspective might itself be limited relative to something vastly greater and more wise and powerful and creative than we. Are we the most sublime reality of all existence? Or is there an ocean beyond us that we might have little inkling of? That, in a nutshell, pictures what might be learned by a humble attitude in theology and science.

13. Some aspects of reality may be unknown to us simply because we have never thought to invest time and resources to try to learn. An expectant sense of humility can be a motivation toward a spirit of adventure. Inquisitiveness, curiosity and an enjoyment of ambitious dreams can be fruitful. Without such qualities of mind we might never even think that we could explore vast possibilities.

14. Perhaps one of the reasons that so many intelligent people have lost hope in the concept of theology has to do with the fundamental problem cited above—that human concepts may have fundamental limitations in knowing about an infinite divinity. Indeed, the sheer variety of opinions concerning the nature of god should give us pause to consider that many religious or theological systems may largely present metaphors and analogies appropriate to our limited humanness and to our varied cultural contexts. We might admit humbly that many and diverse theologies, though seeming foreign to us, may contain valuable insights about divinity that could complement our own. Perhaps there is deep insight in the proverbial image of the blind men attempting to describe an elephant. No one has a sense of the whole, only a part, yet each may imagine that he comprehends the whole.

15. To seek to persuade all people to believe in one perspective would be a great tragedy. The wide diversity of faiths and theologies is a precious aspect of the richness of religion despite the fact that from a scientific point of view it can seem flawed and relativized. What is needed may be creative interaction and competition in a spirit of mutuality, respect and shared exploration. Were a drab uniformity to be accepted, the possibility of spiritual progress would be diminished. Learning to live with and learn from a rich multiplicity of spiritual perspectives is a step forward, because the more we know, the more we know we do not know. This helps give life creativity and joy. In fact, in order to grow, should we daily become more humble and honest in

admitting how very little we yet comprehend? A humble admission of ignorance and a welcoming of a free and open array of many visions, competing, interacting and influencing each other, may be what best produces progress, what keeps humankind searching, what makes life as we know it more exciting, challenging and progressive.

16. Science is progressively unveiling astonishing aspects of physical reality which have deep, subtle, complex and often mathematical structures which even the most brilliant scientific thinkers have not yet been able to grasp fully, even after centuries of research involving many thousands of geniuses. Might the impressive, seemingly endless depths of this cosmic reality hold yet further mysteries and insights, including areas which relate to what people have thought about divinity, such as concepts of love, creativity, gratitude, purpose, thanksgiving and so forth?

17. Gaining knowledge is like working a quarry. As we chip out bits of information, the mining face gets larger and larger. The more knowledge we gain, the more we can see the extent of the unknown. As we grow in knowledge, we grow in humility. This may be just as true in studying the soul as in the investigations pursued by natural sciences.

18. Should people pursing a humble way to god want to research questions like the following?

1) Is god billions of stars in the Milky Way, and yet is god much more?
2) Is god billions of billions of stars in other galaxies, and yet is god much more?
3) Are time and space and energy all part of god, and yet is god much more?
4) Is god six billion people on Earth and much more?
5) Might god encompass untold billions of intelligences on planets of billions of other stars and yet much more?

6) Can humans who experience three dimensions plus time yet comprehend only a little part of god's possible multitude of dimensions?

7) Is god ultimately the only reality—all else being fleeting shadow and imagination from our very limited five senses acting on our tiny brains?

8) Is god just beginning to create his universes and allows each of his children to participate in some small ways in this accelerating creative evolution?

9) Is god the infinitely large and also the infinitely small? Is god each of our inmost thoughts, each of our trillions of bodily cells and each of the billions of wave patterns which are each cell? And yet is he vastly more?

10) Is god all of you, and are you a little part of him?

19. Maybe enthusiasm for worship and adoration of god can be multiplied when we no longer limit god to one tribe or one species or one planet but rather humbly search for unlimited love and purpose and creativity vastly beyond limited ancient human concepts.

20. Throughout history, have gods created by human minds been too small? God concepts typically follow anthropological typologies. Often theological constraints are derived by expanding human analogies, as in the very important arguments against the existence of god based on the problem of evil. These considerations are profoundly important for theology and more generally for belief in god. However, they presuppose a framework of analysis based on limited human understanding. Yet, god may work in mysterious ways, ways beyond our limited concepts. Might what appears to us as god's inhumanity be part of a more perfect picture that we simply cannot see? Divine love may not be so small or simplistic as our limited concepts might suppose.

21. Is it an awesome mystery that evolution has provided us with the mental ability to think about our creator? As far as we know, only humans among all of god's creatures on earth now have the ability to think about god. But are all concepts we can form limited by our five senses and by the smallness of our minds? Therefore can we never totally know god? We really know only our attempts to know god. We devise theologies hoping they in some way adequately represent god. And yet they are always inadequate. If god were small enough to fit our human reason, he would not be god at all but only a better human. Human comprehension is very limited, just as radio receivers that can receive music, voices and wonderful sounds from hundreds of sources but are hopelessly blind to the sunsets and flowers. Would a god small enough to be fully comprehended by human minds be just a product of human minds?

22. Humans have unique mental abilities to study other forms of life on our planet. Because humans' ability to create and to understand appears vastly greater than that of any other kind of earthly creature, have we conceived of ourselves as made in the image of god? Perhaps our freedom and our creativity and spiritual intimations and propensity do provide small windows of insight looking toward divinity. Is it important to imagine such concepts not as capturing god, but as only reasons for enthusiasm to learn more?

23. Many religions hold that knowledge about god comes not from human reasoning but from revelation when god chooses to reveal himself to us. Among other examples, The Church of Jesus Christ of Latter Day Saints, for instance, is based on revelation, translated in 1828 from books of gold. In the Islamic tradition, the Prophet Muhammad (A.D. 570-632) received revelations which were memorized and later written down by his disciples. Christians believe god came into the world two thousand years ago and revealed himself in the life of Jesus of Nazareth.

24. The concept of revelation of course is an extremely important one for theology and religion. However, must it, too, necessarily carry limitations by its very nature? It is in the form of communication to humans and therefore, in a sense, has been limited to what humans at that time could grasp. Humans could write down only what they understood. The concept of communication implies linkage to the mental development of the messengers receiving that communication. Suppose, for the sake of argument, that god had wished two thousand years ago to reveal a modern set of complex scientific ideas describing the cosmos, say, the general theory of relativity, then who would have had the ability even to know the symbols and concepts necessary to have been able to write the theory down even in its simplest form? By this simple example can we see that revelation can have limiting aspects which are dependent on the cultural context within which that revelation is made? Perhaps god is ready to reveal himself more and more with time. Perhaps by research, each generation can be able to comprehend a little more. Over 90% of our concepts about divine creativity have become known only in the 20th century as scientific researches have progressed spectacularly. Nuclear physicists, geneticists and astronomers are demonstrating every week an astonishing richness of accumulating new insight. The pace of this learning is astonishing and speaks to what we might call the depth of creation. As this "depth" is increasingly plumbed by science, can theologians and religious people more generally benefit from some of this extraordinary momentum? If so, could it be very fruitful to find out how? Will we need to work hard on cultivating open-mindedness to have any hope of success?

25. There are clear biblical bases in scriptures of various religions for advocating the need for an inquiring and open mind. For example, according to St. Luke, Jesus said, "Ask, and it shall be given to you;

seek, and you shall find; knock, and it shall be opened to you. For everyone who asks, receives, and he who seeks, finds; and to him who knocks, it shall be opened" (Luke 11:9–10 NASB).

26. Maybe god reveals himself where he finds an inquiring mind—an open mind. For example, in the Acts of the Apostles St. Paul said:

> The God who made the world and everything in it . . . made from one, every nation of mankind . . . that they should seek God, if perhaps they grope for and find Him, though He is not far from each of us; for in Him we live and move and exist, as even some of your own poets have said, "For we also are his offspring." (Acts 17:24, 26, 27–28 NASB)

27. Christian theologians say Christ came to reveal god to us. But because of the limitations of human minds and human language, maybe less than one-hundredth part has been handed down to us.

28. Is it an enthusiasm-building notion to consider the possibility that god may want to reveal himself further than he has done to date through any religion? God may be ever ready to give us new revelation if we will but open our minds to seek and inquire. Developments in understanding both cosmology and evolutionary biology have helped us to realize that the world in which we live is a world of continuous ongoing diverse creativity. Knowledge also works this way. Can spiritual growth do so as well?

29. Time, space and energy comprise the limits of our being and define limits upon our knowledge. God, of course, is not bound by these limits. An aspect of god is as creator of the awesome vastness and complexity of this cosmos. Maybe he knows each person's most fleeting thought just as he knows the power of a quasar and the intricate complexity of each chain of DNA. It is encouraging to realize that the most complicated object that we are now aware of in our universe is the human brain with its as yet mysterious property of inner emergent

consciousness. Consciousness combined with intelligence and an extensive capacity for memory makes us "us." It provides us with the basis for being free agents with the ability to communicate, to know and interact with other similar persons and therefore to live in communities and participate in shared knowledge and activities, to be creative individually and to love, to dream, to hope and also to have deep and abiding spiritual desires and potential. We are not aware yet of how this aspect of reality arises within what biologically is simply a special form of flesh. Yet further research on this reality may provide some of the deepest insights into the nature and purpose of the cosmos. Is it amazing that these minds, which have evolved within the cosmos, seem to have the capacity to interpret the cosmos and to search for its deepest questions, such as How did it develop? How did it form? and even possibly Why does it exist at all? Maybe this is not a meaningless connection? Some have interpreted the situation of the arising of our conscious minds in the cosmos as a blind cosmic accident. According to this way of thinking, some think that our obvious desire to search for divinity and for ultimate meaning and significance is simply a form of anthropomorphizing error—the so-called pathetic fallacy—a human tendency to envision the world in the shape of our own image. However, others see the arising of our minds in the cosmos as being the outcome of fine tuning in ways that physicists are only beginning to explore. If this is true, then it may not be implausible to consider, as Freeman Dyson put it so memorably, that the universe in a way "knew we were coming." Such notions have theological significance and in general lead us to consider the idea that perhaps the capacities of our minds have rather important potential in the grand scheme of things. With such a possibility would come great responsibility. For if what we do with our minds is related importantly to the meaning of the whole cosmos, then surely we might be enthusiastic to find out more.

30. Thus in a spirit of open-minded and hopeful humility, should we try to be continually exploring possibilities to develop our minds and our spiritual capacities, especially by researching more about our creator and the creator's purpose for us? Perhaps in the astonishing capacity of our minds and in the spiritual hunger that so many people can describe vividly, we have some form of a link or a bridge whereby some human minds may resonate with the mind of god in various subtle ways. For example, people of Christian upbringing may recall that St. Paul wrote in 1 Corinthians 2:9–12 (NEB):

> But, in the words of Scripture, "Things beyond our seeing, things beyond our hearing, things beyond our imagining, all prepared by God for those who love him", these it is that God has revealed to us through the Spirit. For the Spirit explores everything, even the depths of God's own nature. Among men, who knows what a man is but the man's own spirit within him? In the same way only the Spirit of God knows what God is. This is the Spirit that we have received from God, and not the spirit of the world, so that we may know all that God of his own grace has given us.

31. Are we privileged to be so wonderfully made to have minds arising out of bodies that allow us to move and sense and participate in the rich reality that surrounds us? In a sense it is true that the human body is physically far more awe-inspiring even than the stars. Recall again that astronomers now think that the Milky Way galaxy contains roughly one hundred billion stars and that the visible universe contains perhaps roughly as many as one hundred billion other galaxies. Thus the number of stars estimated to be present within what is known as the visible universe is truly astonishing: ten to the power of twenty-two. Yet, the number of atoms in your body is vastly greater than the stars in the universe, by a factor of more than ten thousand.

32. Now if we consider the complexity of the brain, the astonishing aspect of what it is to be a living human being shows itself to be a nontrivial matter. Consider the astronomer Carl Sagan's description of the human brain:

> If each human brain had only one synapse—corresponding to a monumental stupidity—we would be capable of only two mental states. If we had two synapses, then $2^2 = 4$ states, and, in general, for N synapses, 2^N states. But the human brain is characterized by some 10^{13} synapses. Thus the number of different states of a human brain is 2 raised to this power, that is multiplied by itself ten trillion times. This is an unimaginably large number. Partly because of this immense number of functionally different configurations of the human brain no two humans, even identical twins raised together, can ever be really very much alike. These enormous numbers may also explain something of the unpredictability of human behavior. The answer must be that all possible brain states are by no means occupied; there must be an enormous number of mental configurations that have never been entered or even glimpsed by any human being in the history of mankind. From this perspective, each human being is truly rare and different and the sanctity of individual human lives is a plausible ethical consequence.[1]

33. Thus, if as humans we continually surprise ourselves, should we not be prepared to be surprised by the awesome vastness and unknown abilities of god?

34. So what is it we are to be humble about? Our experience of god, our experience of ourselves? Perhaps the experience of god that we overlook most easily is the experience of him through science. Being humbled before science is a good first step toward the humility we should have before divinity. As Vannevar Bush puts it:

> Science here does things. It renders us humble and it paints a universe in which the mysteries become highlighted, in which con-

straints on imagination and speculation have been removed, and which becomes ever more awe-inspiring as we gaze . . . on the essential and central core of faith. Science will be the silence of humility not the silence of disdain.[2]

35. Just as we need the humility to live with conflicting scientific theories, do we also need the humility to accept conflicting religious concepts and attitudes? Friedrich Schleiermacher wrote in 1799, "Nothing is more unchristian than to seek uniformity in religion." He argues that instead of being segregated behind ecclesiastical walls, differences of opinion should be allowed lovingly to work upon, enrich and define each other. He claimed that lack of appreciation for other religions has no basis in religion itself. The more adequately one learns about the infinite, the more humility and openness one will have for the unlimited range of divine manifestations.

36. Maybe the creator's plan, not only for the physical universe but also for the metaphysical, is ever-increasing revelation, growth, change, complexity, variety and creativity.

37. All readers of this humble book are lovingly invited to send to the Templeton Foundations varieties of suggestions on ways science research might expand human understanding of divinity and possibilities for humans to help with divine purposes.

CHAPTER THREE

What Benefits from Humility?

1. As we have seen, humility can be an important gateway to developing a deeper understanding of reality, whether in science or in theology. A purpose of this chapter is to consider the benefit of humility in helping to reduce disputes and wars by religious people.

2. Most major religions of the world teach that to grow in spirituality, we need to be humble in our approach to worshiping. After all, the typical posture of worship is that of humility and reverence before the divine. If we free ourselves of self-will and surrender to divine will, as is often taught, then we can become channels for divine love and wisdom to flow to others.

3. It can be a religious virtue reverently to cherish scriptural beliefs and to study them with the utmost seriousness. But of course a reverse side of this virtue can be a vice of intolerance. Is it easy to become intolerant if we are not diligent to guard our minds actively to be humble and to remember that despite differences in religious traditions we all have profoundly limited concepts with respect to the vast divine realities? Can love and the vastness of divinity reduce our differences as we seek to understand by a variety of different ways and through many various traditions? Can diligence in humility help heal conflict between many communities holding different religious points of view?

4. Some communists and other people have thought the best remedy for the differences and wars between religions is to ignore all religion. The term atheism of course refers to an intellectual belief that denies the possibility of the existence of god. That concept is often associated with a focus on rational maturity and stoical intellectual courage. Also, atheism has been associated with the philosophies of materialism, or positivism, which are based on the conviction that one should only speak about or take seriously concepts which are empirically well defined. Atheism often has a cultural context as well. It may result from a rejection of some particular view of god. For example, atheism can mean rejecting the picture of a "white-bearded old king above the sky" recalled from childhood days.

5. Because such small concepts of divinity may not seem to fit with facts observed even by scientists, atheists deny that divinity exists. How egotistical is a person who says, "If god does not conform to my thoughts, then he does not exist"? Perhaps then atheism as a philosophy may need some humility of its own. For it is one thing not to have seen something or not to have rationally explained something and quite another to claim an impossibility proof. As the cell biologist Lewis Thomas has written, "The greatest of all the accomplishments of twentieth-century science has been the discovery of human ignorance." The possibility of divinity will always haunt the materialist and positivist with doubt about the logic of their faith in certainty.

6. Some people have said that religion causes wars and that the diversity of religious beliefs will always be divisive. But probably such wars were not primarily religious in nature. History reveals that great havoc and suffering were caused not by religion but by people who thought their own concept of god was the only one worthy of belief.

7. Pride was the first of the seven deadly sins enumerated by St. Gregory. Any verbal and physical violence in religions could be reduced

when people claim not a monopoly on truth but rather an enthusiasm to search diligently for ever more spiritual information. Ralph Waldo Trine has said:

> Let us not be among the number so dwarfed, so limited, so big-oted as to think that the infinite God has revealed himself to one little handful of his children, in one little quarter of the globe, and at one particular period of time.[3]

8. A peace-generating possibility at the heart of fruitful religion is the willingness to seek truths in other religions. The Persian scriptures claim, "Whatever road I take joins the highway that leads to thee. . . . Broad is the carpet god has spread, and beautiful the colors he has given it." Buddhist scriptures say "the pure man respects every form of faith. My doctrine makes no difference between high and low, rich and poor; like the sky, it has room for all, and like the water, it washes all alike." A Chinese sage has said, "The broad-minded see the truth in different religions; the narrow-minded see only the differences." And a Hindu holy man has written that only the narrow-minded ask, "Is this man a stranger, or is he of our tribe? But to those in whom love dwells, the whole world is but one family." Lastly, Christian scriptures say: "Are we not all children of one father? God hath made of one blood all nations to dwell on the face of the earth" (Acts 17:26 KJV).

9. Differing concepts of divinity have developed in different cultures. Should anyone say that god can be reached by only one path? Such exclusiveness lacks humility because it presumes that a human can comprehend the fullness of truth. The humble person is ready to admit and welcome the various manifestations of unlimited divinity.

10. Jesus quoted Isaiah thus: "But in vain they do worship me; teaching for doctrine the commandments of men" (Matthew 15:9 KJV). Is schism in religions caused by intolerance; and is intolerance a

form of egotism? However, tolerance is not the same as the humble approach. Can we seek to benefit from the inspiring highlights of other denominations and religions, not just to tolerate them? Should we try our very best to give the beauties of our religions to others, because sharing our most prized possessions enhances the highlights of each? An old Chinese precept is, "The good man does not grieve that other people do not recognize his merits. His only anxiety is lest he should fail to recognize theirs." It is a mistake for people of different religions to try to agree with each other. The result may be not the best of each but rather the watered-down, least-common denominator.

11. More fruitful can be a spirit of humility in which we recognize that no one will ever comprehend all that divinity is. Therefore, let us permit and encourage each researcher or prophet to proclaim the best as it is revealed to each. There is no conflict unless the restrictive idea of exclusiveness enters in. We can hold our ideas of the gospel with the utmost enthusiasm, while humbly admitting that we know ever so little of the whole and that there is plenty of room for those who think they have understood reality in a different way. The evil arises only if one prophet forbids his audience to listen to any other prophet. The conceit and self-centeredness of such restriction—the false pride of saying that god can be only what we have learned him to be—should be obvious. By long endurance each religion gives evidence of its benefits, so should not worshipers of all faiths be wholeheartedly grateful when other faiths offer to share with us the beautiful treasures of their tradition?

12. Has the human ego been the cause of religious splits, fractions and even denominations for thousands of years? In every major religion, have wars been fought about differences of creeds? Have nations or tribes rejected or persecuted or exterminated others because they worshiped different gods or the same god as taught by different reli-

gious leaders? This is human ego run wild. Let us humbly admit how very small is the measure of human minds. This realization helps to prevent religious conflicts and can remove a sometimes reasonable basis for criticisms by atheists against religion. Moreover, can humility of this kind open more minds to the idea that science can illuminate religion? If theology is approached through humility, then possibly some sciences can help religions to research basic invisible realities. Can this open the door for a variety of scientific research to begin to give us over 100 fold more spiritual information to supplement all the wonderful ancient scriptures and revelations?

13. If people concentrate only on their own progress or enlightenment, are they essentially self-centered? Instead, should they also help others and share what has been learned with others by speaking, writing, broadcasting and disseminating various ideas? Should such new evangelists be welcomed and respected for their generosity?

14. Influenced by humanism, sometimes clergy in churches, mosques and synagogues unknowingly encourage religious strife as a by-product of working for political or social goals rather than purely spiritual ones. Some may strive too much to create an earthly, material, manmade kingdom separate from the spiritual, internal kingdom that Jesus emphasized. In some nations, for example, have religious groups sometimes encouraged armed force by governments (or even violence by terrorists) for the sake of social justice? Some neglect to teach their members that enduring improvement should begin with self-improvement and voluntary improvements in our own hearts. Compulsory brotherhood is a contradiction in terms.

15. Many people of all faiths show evidence of spiritual growth. Matters of the spirit do not appear to have been monopolized by one doctrine or one religion. Theodore Parker taught that the doctrinal formulations of Christianity have changed and will change from age to

age and what is sometimes called heresy at one time is accepted as orthodox and infallible doctrine in another age. Old forms, Parker says, give way to new, and each new form will capture some of the truth but not the whole. "Transient things form a great part of what is taught as religion. An undue place has often been assigned for ceremony, forms and doctrines, while too little study is devoted to the divine life of the soul, love to God and love to man."[4]

16. Religious advance overall seems to spring from deep humility and search. Therefore, it comes most easily to people who are aware of their ignorance and their need to learn.

17. Intellect, wealth and impressive education often seduce people into self-reliance. All of these can be blessings. But humility is needed to counteract temptation to pride. We are all tempted and need to be reminded of deeper, greater realities beyond ourselves and upon which we depend totally. Of course, some theologians do know over ten times as much about religious histories, creeds and rituals as the average layperson or minister. But if they claim to have more than 1% of the knowledge of god, are they not pitiful in their pride? St. Paul said:

> Make no mistake about this: if there is anyone among you who fancies himself wise—I mean by the standards of this passing age—he must become a fool to gain true wisdom. For the wisdom of the world is folly in God's sight. Scripture says, "He traps the wise in their own cunning"; and again, "The Lord knows that the arguments of the wise are futile." So never make mere men a cause for pride. (1 Corinthians 3:18–21 NEB)

18. Human ego often makes people try to solve problems by human effort alone without turning to seek assistance in god's wisdom. Can rigid creed be a form of pride if it means we think we understand all about god? Both the Old and New Testaments are critical of the proud. "Every one that is proud in heart is an abomination to the

Lord," it says in Proverbs (Proverbs 16:5 KJV), and St. James warned that "God resisteth the proud, but giveth grace unto the humble" (James 4:6 KJV). "A man's pride shall bring him low: but honor shall uphold the humble in spirit" (Proverbs 9:23 KJV). "Pride goeth before destruction, and a haughty spirit before a fall" (Proverbs 16:18 KJV). "By humility and the fear of the Lord are riches, and honor, and life" (Proverbs 22:4 KJV). "With the lowly is wisdom" (Proverbs 11:2 KJV). "Humble yourselves in the sight of the Lord, and he shall lift you up" (James 4:10 KJV).

19. Sometimes large councils of churches make exclusive dogmatic pronouncements, even in fields where they are poorly informed, such as science, economics or politics. Can this create even more division, hatred or strife than they intended to reduce? Would results be better if they expressed love for all, welcomed diversity and avoided the sin of self-righteousness?

20. Becoming unselfed opens the door to communication with god. One who relies on his or her own wisdom or beauty or skill or money shuts god out. But one who is humble and grateful for such god-given blessings opens the door to heaven on earth here and now. For each of us to grow in spirituality, should we be humble in worshiping divinity? Should we free ourselves of self-will and surrender to god's will? If we get rid of ego-centeredness, we can become clear channels for god's love and wisdom to flow through us, just as sunlight pours through an open window.

21. Science possibly can help religious thinkers to consider a reality-focused model of knowing in which what we think we know is tested vigorously and is developed by trying as hard as possible to learn about realities that are external to our own selves, to our interests and egos. Like other people, scientists vary greatly in whether their personal character is either humble or arrogant. A scientist can hardly be

successful over the long term without being humble before the external realities which provide the enduring basis for his success in making discoveries. Even in purely mathematical innovation, often the mathematician feels like a discoverer and has the sense that the source of deep mathematical ideas lies outside of his specific mental abilities. In ways as yet unknown, mathematicians often will speak of the origination of their breakthroughs in a sense as if the concepts enter the mind as a kind of revelation which is made possible by mathematical talent but not ultimately reducible only to it.

22. As we have seen earlier, it may be possible for many scientists and theologians to assist one another in a spirit of mutual excitement over exploring reality both in its purely physical aspects as well as in its more ultimate or spiritual aspects. Clearly, serious commitment to humility would be needed on both sides for such a dynamism to develop without one group seeking to reduce the significance of the other's expertise and point of view. Some prospects are already quite encouraging, such as in medical science, where increasingly researchers find that religion can have important beneficial effects on health. More and more healing and health are being seen as involving a partnership between inner resources of mind and spirit and external scientific medicine. Such a vision treats the whole person and also avoids unnecessary conflicts. Why not learn from what is best in each field that can be demonstrated by objective methods rather than doctrinal disputes? Surely we can learn to transcend an either/or perspective so that we can welcome all types of remedies and prevention whose benefits can be verified.

23. It is typical of groups involved in any cause, whether sacred or secular, that if they begin to believe they have the answer, then the movement ossifies. It seems that the universe has been constructed in such a way by god that its creative principle is linked with movement, change, innovation and growth. Those who are sure they already have

the answers may gradually become obsolete. Perhaps built-in obsolescence is god's plan for keeping the world of ideas forever young, fresh,
invigorating and multiplying. The self-confident proud grow old and
die, and usually so do their rigid ideas.

24. To best deal with conflicts over dogmatism, possibly we can
benefit most by listening carefully and respectfully rather than arguing.
If a message is not truth, it will fade away in time and especially if made
to compete in the open air with other more broad-minded ideas. The
open-minded approach to religion is to look for god in a multitude of
ways and wherever possible to engage in the kind of empirical questioning pursued by scientists.

25. It is likely that we all will benefit if we learn to enjoy the give
and take of debate or disagreement in a humble mode of thinking where
we admit we are all seeking, where we hope to be on the right track but
recognize that perhaps we are not, and if so, then all the better if we
change our thinking (and thanks very much indeed to our critics for the
help). Progress thrives in the context of fair and fully open competition.
God gave us the benefit of having the magnificent capacity of creative
freedom. It is a common unfortunate habit of groups in power to try to
stifle this free creativity and to enforce drab conformity and uniformity.
This generally fails everybody over the long term, as has been demonstrated over and over. We know that humans flourish best in a system of
life that stimulates novelty, innovativeness and individuality and that
rewards new approaches, new concepts, new inventions and new and
better ways of thinking about life and its ultimate ends and concerns.
This simple principle can be applied in many domains with great success—in business, in government, in religion, and so forth. New discoveries come most productively from free minds. The worship of God is
not weakened by open mindedness any more than cosmology was weakened when the Ptolemaic worldview was replaced by that developed by

Copernicus. It is a novel concept, but maybe one of the purposes of god is progress. This may touch upon a deep mystery: the purpose of freedom and the openness of creativity in the cosmos. If the cosmos and our own minds have this capacity, then maybe our activities have great usefulness and great potentiality in the creator's designs. Possibly divine design appears in our own freedom more than in any cosmically enforced order, such as many religious thinkers have presumed in the past when they conceived of god as having attributes of a wise king.

26. By learning humility, we find that the purpose of life on earth may be far different from what anyone now supposes. Diligently, each child of god can seek to find out and obey divine purposes. If we encourage free and friendly competition of ideas, the truth may emerge more easily. It may be the divine plan that any organization that tries to maintain its truth as the status quo is headed for extinction. No matter how well protected, every willow tree grows old and dies. But if, before it dies, a little limb is snipped and put in good moist soil, it will take root, flourish and grow into another tree.

27. This principle seems to apply to plants, animals, people, nations, churches, and even to ideas. From a little sprig of an idea, the world's great bodies of thought grew year by year toward maturity. For example, despite harsh persecution, the early Christian church grew rapidly like a young willow tree for five centuries. Likewise, for five centuries the ideas of Muhammad swept the world like wildfire. Which religions and denominations are growing most rapidly today? Many with the most rapid growth are those that are still young, still exploring, still taking risks, still experimenting with the meaning and purpose of life.

28. Secular ideas and institutions often show this tendency toward the life cycle. Communism, for example, captured a quarter of the world's people in one century for many reasons, in great part due to its

youthful promise to sweep away the stifling patterns of older societies. But in many nations, socialism and communism became so restrictive and coercive that a growing number of dissidents refused to tolerate them. People criticize or leave their countries for other places that permit and encourage free expression of thought.

29. Whether youthfulness is an important principle of life considered from a biological or spiritual viewpoint, the young at heart and the young in mind are humble and open-minded and welcome new ideas. Jesus' admonition to become like little children may have been his way of telling us to experiment, explore new ideas, test things, admit our lack of knowledge and know-how and be humble. Yes, change and progress require searching and youthful attitude. Ideas and institutions which remain rigid for generations tend to wither.

30. Christians think god appeared in Jesus of Nazareth two thousand years ago for our salvation and education. But should we take it to mean that education and progress stopped there, that Jesus was the end of change, the end of time? Is such notion compatible with the divine, free, open, creative nature of the universe? To say that god cannot reveal himself again in a decisive way because he did it once centuries ago can seem sacrilegious. Should we be gentle, kind and sympathetic toward new prophets even though they bring new ideas strange to us? Should laws forbid religious expression and research, however misguided we think them to be? Was any useful purpose served when the Inquisition forced Galileo to recant in 1633? Jesus, too, was considered unorthodox by the learned religious establishment of his day. Beneficial originators in other great religions also were often called heretics. Abraham and Moses were considered heretics by neighboring tribes in their age. Should those with the humble approach invite the new researchers to share with us all what they think they have learned by speaking, writing, broadcasting and publishing their ideas?

31. Just as each tree or child or soul can grow in the correct nourishing environment, so too can the world-soul of humanity grow and flourish if we encourage global research, toleration and inquiry? Religious leaders in every nation can seek to increase spiritual understanding just as quickly as research scientists increase our understanding of the physical world. Much, of course, depends upon our willingness to love those who are different from ourselves even though they investigate strange and new ideas. As Ella Wheeler Wilcox put it:

> A thousand creeds have come and gone
> But what is that to you or me:
> Creeds are but branches of a tree
> The root of Love lives on and on.

32. Humbly to admit that we know only a very little of god's limitless reality does not make us agnostic. If medical doctors can admit with an open mind that they do not understand all diseases, symptoms and cures, can we be equally humble and honest, not agnostic, by admitting we each have vastly more to learn about divinity? Should we brand every person with new spiritual research as a godless materialist, any more than we would have any scientists accuse every believer of being a dogmatic roadblock to progress? There is room for many branches on the tree. The lifesap of pure unlimited love lives on and on.

CHAPTER FOUR

Creation
Through Change

1. Increasing evidence indicates that creation is just beginning. Are humans just starting to understand that we may have been given creative talents possibly so we can become helpers in a divine accelerating creative process? Are the old ways of structuring and ordering institutional religions adequate for future progress? Can concepts or rituals sometimes be too rigid, too traditional? Can new, freer, more entrepreneurial and adaptable concepts be helpful supplements to ancient revelations so that man's god-given mind may help spiritual information to increase over 100 fold?

2. As we have seen earlier, biological evolution seems to show an overall tendency toward increased complexification. The challenges humans now face are reminiscent of concepts promoted by the scientist-Jesuit visionary Teilhard de Chardin, a professional paleontologist. Particularly, he was involved in research on the evolution of modern humans. He asked fundamental questions about the voluntary process, especially where it is going—or perhaps more precisely what are its potentialities and *where could it go* if humans followed a beneficent vision of spiritual aspiration and possibility. He suggested that humanity faced the possibility of making remarkable progress toward what he called "the sphere of spirit." Perhaps this remains one of the greatest ques-

tions we face as the 21st century begins. Does the astonishing creativity of the world and of ourselves within it signify a sphere of possibility that might flourish were we to consider humbly what our role could be in a quest to comprehend and follow sublime purposes?

3. Although we seem to be the most sophisticated species at present on our planet, perhaps we should not think of our place as at the end of cosmogenesis. Should we resist the pride that might tempt us to think that we are the final goal of creation? Possibly, we can become servants of creation or even helpers in divine creativity. Possibly, we are a new beginning, the first creatures in the history of life on earth to participate consciously in the ongoing creative process.

4. Does the world urgently need to study basic spiritual realities? Do theologians need to be humble and open-minded? Leaders may be tempted to think that conformity and control are required for the orderliness of religion and for faithfulness. Most religions have developed creeds, doctrines, dogmas, liturgy and hierarchies of laypeople and clergy. Order and tradition of course do help groups to live as an organization of people whose ideals are compatible and link together the generations in mutual ideals. However, because of a lack of humility, have we observed throughout the history of most religions a tendency for dogma or hierarchy to stifle progress? If the members and clergy become more humble, could they re-form dogma in a more open-minded and inquiring way as a beginning point for continual improvements?

5. As Jaroslav Pelikan has remarked with much wisdom, tradition at its best should reflect a living spirit of worshipful celebration of the best of the past aimed at creating a wholesome lively future. Should we praise the "living faith of the dead, not the dead faith of the living"? If a family (or a corporation or church) prepares a good budget but never changes it for a century, such a budget will surely become obsolete and gradually change from being a help to being a millstone hung round

the family's neck. Budgets are helpful only if they are continually revised and improved. Like budgets, can church structures and creeds be more helpful if they are continually reexamined and improved? John Calvin taught that "to be Reformed is to be always reforming."

6. Throughout history has religion developed and progressed often by the work of those who were first regarded as heretics? The Pharisees were learned, deeply devoted and sincerely holy men, but most of them seemed to have regarded Jesus as a heretic. Others once called heretics were Buddha, Paul, Zoroaster, Muhammad, Wycliffe, Hus, Luther, Calvin, Wesley, Fox, Smith, Emerson, Bahaullah and Eddy. Christians believe god was incarnated into the world as a human. However, note that Jesus was not a traditionalist urging restudy of Abraham and Moses. Rather, he was an innovator who proclaimed and taught new revelation. Rarely does a historian or conservative become a hero of later history. Many of history's most creative people have been untraditional, far-reaching thinkers who seek to improve accepted customs of their time. Often such people have been called radicals.

7. But only later their contributions are recognized and celebrated. Ironically, traditionalists then remember them as the founders of the tradition. This has happened, for example, to the leaders of the American revolution—the founding fathers. But it is good to realize that they were risk-taking innovators once, whose open-mindedness allowed them to envision a new and better way of life and to act accordingly. If people want to serve as leaders and innovators, it is helpful to be humble enough to foresee that what may seem firm or fixed habit and tradition may in the long view be seen to have been a passing impediment to progress.

8. For humanity to progress, should we be eagerly interested to welcome whomever might be the new Columbus, the new Galileo, the new Copernicus? Can creative geniuses enlarge our global vision and

help us to comprehend how tiny and temporary we are and how little we have yet discovered?

9. Dr. Robert Hilliard has estimated that if the growth of knowledge continues at the present rate, then when a baby born today graduates from a university, the quantity of knowledge on earth will be four times as great. By the time such a child is fifty years old, the amount of knowledge will be thirty-two times as great; and 97% of every thing known to human beings will have been learned since the day the child was born. The futurist John Naisbitt is far more bullish on the growth of information. He affirms an estimate that the quantity of information is doubling every thirty months. At such rate of growth the quantity may be one thousand times as great in only twenty-five years, and a million times as great in only fifty years. A focus of this book is to encourage many entrepreneurs trying various methods for spiritual information (such as research on such basic spiritual realities as love, purpose, creativity and intellect) to increase over 100 fold in only one century.

10. This is the blossoming time in human creation. Evolution is accelerating. Progress is accelerating. One of god's great blessings to human beings is change, and the present acceleration of change in the world is an overflowing of this blessing. Should those who love god devote over 1% of income to research for new additional spiritual information to supplement the wonderful ancient scriptures?

11. Perhaps only about one child in a million is born with talents which seem almost superhuman in one or more ways. Why does god's process of evolution produce these rare geniuses on earth? Is it the divine plan that they should help all people to progress? The one in a million who contributes a new idea to humanity can be a blessing to billions, which helps god's creation continue to progress.

12. In addition to the geniuses given more-than-human minds, god also creates saints and prophets gifted with more-than-human souls. A

prophet is a pioneer in the vast uncharted regions of the spirit. For spiritual progress to flourish, do we need to cultivate interest and humility to listen carefully and learn from such people, recognizing their important gifts? If no two persons are equal or identical in body or mind, is it probable that no two persons are equal in spiritual insight? However much we may yearn for equality, it does not seem to be part of the divine plan.

13. Sören Kierkegaard taught that the human race advances on the backs of those rare geniuses who venture into realms of which most of us are afraid. Did Arend van Leeuwin exaggerate by saying, "Ninety-nine percent of people, irrespective of race, play a passive as opposed to a creative role; and even the creative section are passive with regard to ninety-nine percent of their civilization"?[5] And Huston Smith, the masterful chronicler of world religious thought and practice, wrote:

> The average man is no more capable of forming his imagination in ways that resolve his feelings nobly than he is capable of being his own scientist. Both tasks require genius. Geniuses in the art of shaping man's imaginings are artists, philosophers, prophets, and seers. Over time their creations coalesce and distill into cultures. As the religious forms of traditional Judaism and Christianity are losing their powers to inform the contemporary mind, humanity desperately needs religious geniuses who can create new imaginable forms, convincing to the contemporary mind which consummate man's needs for home, vocation, and transcendence.[6]

14. Again, fixity in matters of seeking to know and relate to divinity can be the result of a lack of humility. Do histories of religions give evidence that most traditionalists become eventually hopelessly out of touch with advancing discoveries and that their fixed positions usually pass away? Are fixed dogma and bureaucracy similar? Do both reduce progress? If a purpose of humans on earth everywhere might be to help as "created co-creator" with god, is it not presumptuous or

egotistical for any one group to suppose there to be only one proper way to inspire a person to contribute as a helper in the continuing creativity of the universe?

15. In our own times have we witnessed several brave religious pioneers who have marched into old areas of religious endeavor with a new bold spirit and program? Brother Roger Schutz, the founder of the Taizé community in France, has answered one of the greatest spiritual needs in the postwar world. His quiet monastic community attracts architects, painters, theologians, lawyers and countless professional people who, after submitting themselves to his program of prayer and reflection, return to the world to pursue their careers more fully committed to creating a more fruitful world of love and joy. His efforts to organize the worldwide Council of Youth in 1970 inspired thousands of young people to go to Taizé and then return to their own countries to work for religious renewal.

16. Mother Teresa of Calcutta, often called by people of many faiths a living saint, demonstrated to the world yet another way that divine creativity can be helped through human (or in her case superhuman) effort. Mother Teresa formed a new order of religious women who have lived among and helped the poorest of the poor in India and many other nations to develop fruitful joyful lives through divine love. Public as well as private charitable organizations could follow her example and methods for providing human services and love to the outcasts of our age. Malcolm Muggeridge said about Mother Teresa and her Missionaries of Charity:

> When I think of them in Calcutta, as I often do, it is not the bare house in a dark slum that is conjured up in my mind, but a light shining and a joy abounding. I see them diligently and cheerfully constructing something beautiful for God out of the human misery and affliction that lies around them.[7]

17. Another pioneering woman in the struggle for spiritual renewal in the world is Chiara Lubich. Her Focolare, or Fireside Movement, begun in Italy in 1943, has become a successful international means of providing spiritual community to people for whom the church as a system and institution is not enough. Living in lay communities structured as families and imbued with the loving ethos of family life, architects, doctors, engineers, nurses, carpenters, secretaries and others find a sense of spiritual belonging that run-of-the-mill society does not provide. Her innovative program, now adopted by thousands of people the world over, infuses vigorous inspiration into volunteers who seek to reanimate the world in the spirit of love. Her New Family, New Humanity and New Parishes movements are all creative additions to the traditional concept of church organization.

18. Through spiritual pioneers like Brother Roger, Mother Teresa and Chiara Lubich, can new blessings flow? Should freedom be given to people like these three who take seriously the challenge to be humble co-creators with god? Should their messages be studied worldwide? The next stage of human help in spiritual progress may have much to do with the examples and creativity of dedicated men and women, geniuses of the spirit, who will blaze trails for the rest of us to follow. (To encourage progress of this kind Templeton Foundation Prizes for Progress in Religion were established in 1972. A list of awardees is included at the end of this book, in Appendix Five.)

19. In recent centuries, hundreds of Protestant denominations have been born from new concepts and by breaking free of conformity. Multitudes of cults and sects have arisen in other major religions also. But how many of these sponsor research for more fruitful and testable new ideas?

20. Vannevar Bush was a pioneering electronics engineer, president of The Carnegie Institution, and author of the hugely influential

postwar report to Congress entitled "Science: The Endless Frontier." He wrote that "a faith that is over-defined is the very faith most likely to prove inadequate to the great moments of life."[8] Certainly the great moments of life include those crises in which imaginative expanded concepts are needed. Marceline Bradford has said:

> What is explicit here is the fact that millions of intellectuals the world over have become disenchanted with backward-looking religious institutions. . . . In order to recapture the great thinking minds of the world, the clergy must turn their heads 180 degrees from past to future. With feet planted squarely in the present and eyes directed to the future, religious leaders can find factual bases in science for viable, solid dynamic doctrines. For science and rationality are enemies not of religion—only of dogmatism.[9]

21. Can even the best doctrines function for some as blinders serve on a horse? Can they create a kind of tunnel vision? One unfortunate aspect of dogma is that it tends to belittle the infinite variety and nature of divinity. Dogmas are, after all, written by human beings, and human concepts of god are always limited. Would it be unfortunate and a great waste of human energy if every advance or reform in the church had the nature of being a rival from the outside? Those well-meaning people within the church would naturally be more resistant to outside intrusion, would tend to side with tradition, thus strengthening the forces behind the status quo and ultimately hindering progress.

22. Many religious concepts come directly or indirectly from ancient scriptures. An unavoidable limitation of utilizing such texts as a total basis for contemporary faith is that they were written within a context which may no longer be appropriate for ours today. Recent sciences reveal a universe billions of times larger and older and more complex than the one conceived by the ancients. The creative challenge is to enrich understanding and appreciation for the old with a welcoming

of concepts and perspectives which may represent truly new insights and creative improvements, which can leverage the power of the past into a forward-looking adventure of learning more and more about the wonders of god and his purposes through ongoing creativity. Can it be an inspiring challenge to read the Bible in this way, which can help each generation of god's people to search for far more of divine realities than can ever be contained in the language and thought patterns of any age? Should we not be able to give a fuller and wider interpretation of divine revelation today, now that the range of our understanding of the universe has been so vastly enlarged? Why should we often try to express spiritual truths using obsolete words, limited concepts and ancient thought patterns? If some scholars think that Jesus himself wrote nothing, could this suggest that what he had to teach should not be frozen into words, even in his own age? Thus, he did not limit for future generations their range of spiritual concepts and research.

23. Has god given us free will for new interpretations of eternal truths so that in our limited way we can be creative? But of course, free will gives us also the awesome power to build our own individual hells and heavens here on earth as well as for eternity. God knew free will could lead to problems, evils and much suffering, but the divine plan seems to include that out of adversity we can learn how to create; out of struggle we can become more spiritual. Out of our desire to change the world for the better, will we learn that the principle of creation is change and that through change god's creations will continue and accelerate?

24. In conclusion, we might consider the description of reality given by Harold K. Schilling, a physicist:

> I want to call attention to one more of the fundamental, constitutive characteristics of reality that provides, I feel, a criterion for the acceptability of values. Reality is historical and developmental,

rather than merely inert and fixed; and it is creative and productive, rather than sterile and only conservative; and it is open, rather than closed, to new possibilities, and thrusts toward the future. Reality seems not to have come into being full-blown, but gradually, and over a long period of time.[10]

25. Schilling claims that matter and most likely all other manifestations of reality are fundamentally developmental. He suggests reality is a continuing creative process in an unmistakable direction, "from the simple to the complex, from the small to the large, from the isolated individual entities to combinations and integrated systems, and to community." Do links between people, between churches and between nations need to be forged as a Mother Teresa or a Brother Roger or a Chiara Lubich would forge them? From the study of biology, physics and theology, the long-range cosmic trends seem obvious. In the words of Schilling:

> In any case, it seems clear that if our values are to be in harmony with long-range trends—and divine intent—they must be such as not to hinder or inhibit development and change, and the emergence of the utterly novel, but to facilitate them, and thus to contribute to the building of a mankind and world characterized at its ground by development. [11]

26. When considering the fruitfulness of the notion of creation do we see that possibly the most important aspect of the divine purpose can be realized through ongoing creativity, change and innovation? Do we need to learn ways to embrace change in a manner that does not simply follow whimsy or fashion but instead taps into the deep symphonies of the divine creativity? Beneficial creativity often goes against whimsy and fashion and habit. It often is rigorous. It can be demanding and difficult. Can it be seen best in the lives of rare and extraordinary people? Most importantly, the path followed is not that of the ego

but the quest to follow that which totally and infinitely transcends the ego. For that, great humility is needed.

27. Let none of us have any quarrel with any theologian. Let us happily admit that his or her concepts and doctrines may be right. But let us listen most carefully to any theologian who is humble enough to admit also that he may be wrong—or at least that the door to great insights by others is not closed. Let us seek to learn from each other. Let us try to use sciences to help verify or falsify new concepts. Let us always keep trying many methods to discover over 100 fold more about divinity.

CHAPTER FIVE

When Is a Blossoming Time
of Humanity?

1. Should we be overwhelmingly grateful to have been born in the 20th century? Is the slow progress of prehistoric ages now speeding up? It seems that centuries of human enterprise are now miraculously bursting into flower. Is the development of human knowledge accelerating? Is the present generation reaping the fruits of generations of scientific thought? More than half of the scientists who ever lived are alive today. More than half of the discoveries in the natural sciences have been made from 1900 to 1999. More than half of the goods produced since the earth was born have been produced in the 20th century. Over half of the books ever written were written from 1949 to 1999. More new books are published each month than were written in the entire historical period before the birth of Columbus.

2. Most astronomers believe what we call the visible universe began with a "big bang" some time between ten and twenty billion years ago. Although the nature of that explosive origin remains obscure, many scientists believe it marked the coming into being not only of matter and energy, but of space and time too. For many millions of years the cosmic material expanded as a soup of hot gas, but as gravity worked its inexorable magic, so material was pulled into huge structures that were eventually to become a vast cosmic ocean of billions of galaxies. One such galaxy, the Milky Way, contains our sun, with its ret-

inue of planets. Countless other stars were born, blazed in splendor and faded, long before the sun even existed. Thus much of the history of the universe occurred while, to quote from Genesis, "the earth was without form" (Genesis 1:2 KJV).

3. Radioactive dating indicates that the earth and the other bodies in the solar system were formed about 4.5 billion years ago. Scientists remain unsure of when life began on earth, but fossil microbes found in western Australia and in Swaziland have been dated at 3.5 billion years. For comparison, 3.5 billion minutes ago the year was 1330. The scourge of the Black Death had begun to spread throughout Europe and ultimately killed a fourth of the total population of the continent. It is interesting to note that while single-celled creatures probably first appeared on earth almost 4 billion years ago, it has taken over 85% of the total period of evolution since that time to evolve a creature with *more* than one cell. The oldest known fossils of animals, called *ediacara*, are found in south Australia and have been dated at 560 million years or more ago. The evolutionary diversification into fishes, reptiles and mammals occupied another 500 million years. Hominids did not appear until a few million years ago, while true humans, our species *homo sapiens*, have probably been around for only 100,000 years. For comparison, 100,000 thousand minutes is equivalent to less than 70 days.

4. It has been only six thousand years since mankind invented any form of writing. Thus, only lately has human existence been within the age of written communications, and it has only been this age of writing that has allowed the full flowering of the human intellect. Once again, for comparison, six thousand minutes is only four days.

5. Even then, progress continued to be slow. Ninety-seven percent of recorded human history passed by before humanity began its rapid journey of scientific discovery peering into the secrets of nature. Even

in 1800 there was no faster transportation than the horse on land and sailing ships on the seas. Communications then were scarcely faster than they had been in the days of Moses. Energy still came mostly from muscle power. Electricity was a laboratory curiosity. Germs were unknown. Photography was unheard of. Fewer than a million people on earth could read or write. Ninety-five percent of the workers in the world had jobs in agriculture and fishing, compared with less than 4% in the United States in 1999.

6. As recently as the 16th century Nicholas Copernicus suggested that the earth revolved around the sun. Science in its modern form was founded in the time of Galileo and Newton, in the 17th century. Newton discovered the laws of motion and gravitation and published them in his celebrated book *Principia* in 1687. Not before the middle of the 19th century did James Clerk Maxwell unify electricity and magnetism in a single mathematical theory and prove that light is an electromagnetic wave. Even more recently, electromagnetic waves of other wavelengths were found: radio waves, x-rays, microwaves, infrared and ultraviolet and gamma rays, forming a continuous spectrum. From these discoveries came many familiar forms of modern technology, such as electronics, radar, radio astronomy, television and lasers. At about the same time that Maxwell produced his work on electromagnetism, Charles Darwin and Alfred Wallace published their theory of evolution, introducing into biology the modern concept of progress.

7. The great flourishing of physical science accelerated in pace in the early 20th century. In 1900 Max Planck, while studying the theory of heat, first proposed that electromagnetic radiation is emitted in tiny packets, or quanta. Thus was the quantum theory born. Albert Einstein was able to use Planck's hypothesis to explain the photoelectric effect, the basis of the modern solar cell. The quanta of light became known as photons. Then Niels Bohr applied the quantum idea to

the structure of atoms. By the late 1920s an entirely new quantum mechanics, which applied to the realm of atoms and molecules, was worked out to replace Newton's two-hundred-year-old classical mechanics. This revolutionary theory of the microworld was found to have the most profound implications for the nature of reality and continues to astound scientists today with its bizarre predictions.

8. Meanwhile, another revolution was taking place in humanity's understanding of space and time. Einstein showed that neither distances in space nor intervals of time are absolute and universal but are relative to the state of motion of the observer. His theory of relativity, published in 1905 and extended to include the effects of gravitation in 1915, transformed our picture of the universe on the large scale, and gave us the famous formula $E = mc^2$. From this theory flowed many important ideas, like timewarps, curved space and black holes. It also provided a suitable theoretical framework for the burgeoning subject of cosmology—the overall structure and evolution of the universe.

9. These sweeping theoretical advances were accompanied by equally important experimental discoveries. The existence of atoms, hypothesized since the time of ancient Greece, was finally proved with the discovery of radioactivity in 1896. The first subatomic particle, the electron, was discovered soon afterwards by J. J. Thompson. Earnest Rutherford's experiments with radioactive emissions soon established the structure of the atom, conceived of as a central nucleus surrounded by a swarm of orbiting electrons. Electrons were also found emanating from some radioactive nuclei at close to the speed of light. To understand their behavior, physicists needed to have a theory that combined quantum mechanics with some aspects of the theory of relativity. This was finally formulated by Paul Dirac about 1930. One of the predictions that resulted from Dirac's equations was that for each type of sub-

atomic particle there should exist in nature a corresponding antiparticle. Soon afterwards the antielectron, or positron, was discovered among the products of cosmic rays—high-energy particles that pepper the earth from space.

10. These later developments coincided with the beginning of the great science of nuclear physics. In 1932 James Chadwick found the neutron. With the discovery of the muon in 1936, nuclear physicists began to suspect that the subatomic domain was more complex than they had hoped. Following the Second World War, dozens of new particles were found in cosmic radiation or produced in giant accelerator machines. The pace of discovery became so frenetic that Lawrence Berkeley Laboratory in California began to issue a new list of subatomic particles twice yearly. In 1999, many hundreds of different subatomic and subnuclear particle species have been catalogued, and theorists are busy trying to find a deeper level of structure that will explain their properties. It is astonishing to realize that as recently as 1935 physicists widely believed that all matter was composed of just three particles: electrons, protons and neutrons.

11. With the discovery of new particles came the realization that there are additional forces at work deep in the invisible recesses of matter. When the 20th century began, the only known forces of nature were gravitation and electromagnetism. The development of nuclear physics revealed the existence of two nuclear forces, called weak and strong. The strong force binds protons and neutrons together in the nuclei. Like gravitation, the strong nuclear force is attractive but some 10^{40} times more powerful over the tiny distances inside the nucleus. The weak force plays only a minor role in the structure of the nucleus but is responsible for certain types of particle transformation such as beta decay.

12. Alongside these advances in understanding the microscopic realm came equally impressive developments in the study of the cos-

mos. Astronomy, the oldest science, has been revolutionized just in the last half of the 20th century. Edwin Powell Hubble and others proved for the first time in the 1920s that there are other galaxies far beyond our Milky Way. In 1999, we believe there are over one hundred billion such galaxies. Equally significant, Hubble's observations revealed that the distant galaxies seem to be rushing away from us and each other, so that the universe is in a state of expansion. Spin-off from wartime radar research led Sir Bernard Lovell and others to lay the foundations for the science of radio astronomy, which led to the discovery of pulsars and other unusual cosmic bodies. The use of infrared telescopes and x-ray and gamma ray satellites has extended the window of observation to almost the entire electromagnetic spectrum. As a result, new astronomical discoveries have come thick and fast. Quasars, active galactic nuclei, gamma ray bursters and black holes are among the menagerie of astronomical objects being intensively studied by astronomers. Equally impressive is the information gleaned about the early states of the universe following the big bang. The satellite COBE (Cosmic Background Explorer), launched in 1989, mapped with great sensitivity the pattern of heat radiation left over from the big bang. This afterglow of the cosmic birth bathes the universe at a temperature of 2.7 degrees absolute (about -270°C), and it contains the imprint of any primordial irregularities in the structure of the universe. COBE's data revealed vast agglomerations of matter thought to be the precursors of galactic superclusters.

13. From their extensive observations of the motions of stars and galaxies, astronomers have become convinced that in addition to the luminous material such as stars, the universe contains copious quantities of dark or invisible matter. Some estimates suggest that more than 90% of the cosmos may exist in this mysterious form. There is no lack of candidates for what the dark matter might be: black holes, dim stars,

large planets, cosmic strings and exotic subatomic particles are some of the suggestions. One candidate known to contribute to this unseen material is the neutrino. Predicted by Wolfgang Pauli in 1932, neutrinos are so elusive that they are almost impossible to detect. Traveling at or close to the speed of light, they have no electric charge and interact with ordinary matter through the feeble weak nuclear force. This gives neutrinos incredible penetrating powers. A typical neutrino could penetrate many light years of solid lead. Not surprisingly, it took many years before these particles were definitely identified in the laboratory, emanating from nuclear reactors. In 1999, astronomers study the flux of neutrinos produced by the sun, using enormous underground detectors specially designed to spot fleeting individual interactions with atomic nuclei. Scientists believe that vast quantities of neutrinos were created in the big bang and fill the universe alongside the relic heat radiation. It has been calculated that there should be about a billion neutrinos in the universe for every other particle, yet this vast ocean of subatomic entities goes completely unnoticed by us in daily life. Every second, each of our bodies is penetrated by billions upon billions of neutrinos, with absolutely no effect on us whatsoever. Yet collectively, these cosmic neutrinos might outweigh the stars and help determine the ultimate fate of the material universe.

14. Science has taught us the important lesson that things are not always what they seem. Sometimes phenomena that appear real to us are actually distortions or even tricks of perception perpetrated by our lack of knowledge and limited senses. For example, until Copernicus it was assumed that lying in bed was a relatively motionless experience. This seems obvious to anyone who had ever done it. But Copernicus' discovery that the earth and the planets move around the sun implied that because the earth rotates, so a person sleeping in bed moves eastward at hundreds of miles an hour. The sleeper also flies 1,080 miles a minute in another di-

rection because of the earth's revolution around the sun. But this is not all. The solar system moves around the Milky Way at 162 miles per second in yet a third direction, while the Milky Way galaxy participates in the general expansion of the universe discovered by Hubble, so that relative to some distant galaxies we would appear to be traveling at close to the speed of light. So a sleeper may *seem* to be motionless, but in reality he or she has traveled through the galaxy a distance greater than that to the farthest point on earth in less time than it took to read this page.

15. In spite of the enormous strides made by science and the incredible power of our new instruments to reveal the secrets of the universe, large and small, we must accept in all humility that our knowledge is still limited. We cannot even be sure that the vast universe unveiled to us by our telescopes is all that exists. There may be other regions of the universe far beyond the reach of our instruments having very different properties. It is even possible that entire other universes co-exist in parallel with our own. Also, various intelligences not made of materials may exist around or in us. Such ideas, although highly speculative, have been studied with seriousness by cosmologists and physicists in recent years.

16. Sir Bernard Lovell remarks that the problems of whether the universe is finite or infinite, or how it began and how it will end, remains unresolved. He cautions that "the perspective of these questions and the nature of the possible scientific answers have constantly changed since ancient times."[12] This should be enough to cause all men and women to pause humbly before the majesty and infinity of what Jefferson called "nature and nature's god." Discovery and invention have not stopped or even slowed down. Who can imagine what will be discovered if this acceleration continues? Now even the acceleration of discovery seems to be accelerating. The more we learn about the universe the more humble we should be, realizing how ignorant we have been in the past and how much more there is still to discover.

17. The humble approach described in this book means to cultivate a realistic and receptive attitude before the creator and admit that we are not the center of the universe. The sun does not revolve around us. Our five human senses are able to comprehend only a small portion of the mysteries, forces and spiritual realities surrounding us. Our scientific and technological achievements, while impressive, are nevertheless but a first faltering step on the road to ever greater knowledge of this wonderful cosmos, including its invisible and intangible intelligences and realities.

18. Egotism has been a major cause of many mistaken notions in the past. Egotism caused men to think that the stars and the sun revolved around them. Egotism caused men to think that mankind was as old as the universe. Egotism is still our worst enemy. In fact, things are still not what they seem. Only by becoming humble can we learn more. Forces still undreamed of are probably present around us and in us. And more revelations about god's universe will probably be discovered in the 21st century than in all the millenniums before. Are those who believe only what they see pitifully self-centered and lacking in humility?

19. A classic example of how self-centered egotism can stifle scientific progress is the case of the heliocentric concept of the universe. As Lovell explains, the concept that the sun was the center of the universe afforded "centuries of a comforting philosophical stability in which the Universe was envisaged as made for many by god, who had in the beginning endowed the particles of the Universe with such properties as were necessary for the appropriate inertial motions and gravitational forces." It would not have taken two centuries to challenge this notion, he believed, were it not for the "egocentric conviction that man must be near the center of the universe. Indeed, a retrospective judgment is that the abandonment of the idea of the Sun-centered universe would not have been delayed until the twentieth century but for this egoism of man."[13] In this case, the scientific problem of measuring the distance be-

tween stars was overcome more easily than the psychological and spiritual problem of human self-centeredness. Humility is a gateway to discovery. To learn more, we must first realize how little we already know. The unknown around and in us may be over a thousand times greater than what we now know, despite the myriad discoveries made in the 20th century. Even scientists on the cutting edge of new theories about the universe admit this. Ultimate reality can be vastly more astonishing than the sum of phenomena already observed. More and more, the immensity and complexity of the physical universe points to a nonphysical creator who is infinite.

20. The history of science is full of surprises and demolished confidence. The more humble researchers do not expect to find answers but rather to discover multiplying mysteries. Similarly, the future likely may humble scientists because reality is so deep. Consider that many scientists of the 1880s confidently asserted that but for only a few minor technicalities, they had more or less solved all the fundamental problems of science. The quantum and relativity revolutions soon demolished this egotistical claim. Today few scientists would display such hubris. They readily acknowledge the existence of many unseen phenomena and recognize with enthusiasm the likelihood that major transforming discoveries have yet to be made and can be expected to come as profound and puzzling surprises. In this sense, the modern scientists mostly have learned to become more humble than many of their predecessors. The astonishing journey of 20th-century science seems to be one of entry into a domain of endless wonder. What awe-inspiring surprises will the 21st century bring? By applying rigorous science research on the neglected basic invisible realities, can spiritual information also increase over 100 fold?

21. By adopting the humble approach, some scientists are acknowledging that in spite of tremendous scientific breakthroughs in recent times, there can still be a vast, possibly infinite, amount of knowledge to

be learned. Many accept an infinite divinity as the basis of such infinite body of knowledge. In the words of Thomas Carlyle, they might say:

> All visible things are emblems. What thou seest is not there on its own account; strictly speaking is not there at all. Matter exists only spiritually, and to represent some idea and body it forth.[14]

22. In conclusion, we may reflect on what lessons this extraordinary scientific experience may be able to offer for epistemology more widely considered. The objects which science has typically studied are far simpler than the complexity of any human being, whether child or adult. This is true because of the biological complexity of living beings generally, and also because of the neurological complexity of mammals and lastly, because of the very particular aspect of reflective and openly creative self-consciousness which has emerged as a biological novelty from within the very large scale brain of *homo sapiens*. The spiritual impulse in human beings is part of this progress. It may offer profound insights into the nature of nature itself.

23. So if the typical objects of scientific inquiry (such as stars or electrons or planets or molecules or force fields or ocean currents) are far simpler than a human being, yet still lead us into profound and extraordinarily surprising and humbling mysteries in the depths of nature, then how much more so might be the domain of theology where the intended subject of study is the interaction between human beings and the divine source of all of this wonder and mystery? How feeble must even the most impressive efforts be at developing systematic theologies and conceptual systems which are linked by human effort attempting to grasp the ineffable and infinite and ultimate reality! And how rich and sublime must be that Reality?

24. It may be helpful to conclude with a small vignette of theological science fiction. This will involve a leap of the imagination, but per-

haps a helpful one. Imagine, if you will, that once upon a time some day in the far, far distant future, hundreds of thousands of years hence, there will exist a race of beings whom we might consider to be scientists of the spirit. Let us suppose that their intelligence is perhaps a million times greater than ours, perhaps more. If we could meet such beings, we might consider them to be gods. Nonetheless, this would be an error of perception. Let us suppose that for hundreds of thousands of years this race of beings has been exercising unimaginable brilliance in theological matters. Let us suppose we were to have the opportunity to ask these beings to what degree they thought they had captured the depths of the reality of god. What answer might they offer? It is not an unhelpful question. Will they say they have comprehended as much as one-thousandth the depth of the reality of god? Of course we have no ability even to imagine the answer. But perhaps our experience, if it increases our humility, may suggest that the answer might possibly be No. Perhaps it will be a thousand times No. Of course, we cannot now know the answer to that question. But that, too, is useful to know.

25. The question before us is whether theologians and religious scholars, clergy and laity, can also take the humble approach? If they accept the inexhaustibility of god's revelation in terms of science, as do many scientists, should they hope that revelations in terms of the spirit are also inexhaustible, vastly exceeding our capacities to grasp them? Possibly, the greater part of divine revelation, both scientific and spiritual, may still lie ahead of us, not behind us.

CHAPTER SIX

The Vast Unseen

1. Reflecting on the vast cosmos with its possible infinity of galaxies, the distinguished British astronomer Sir James Jeans asked:

> Do their colossal uncomprehending masses come nearer to representing the main ultimate reality of the universe, or do we? Are we merely part of the same picture as they or is it possible that we are part of the artist? Are they perchance only a dream, while we are brain cells in the mind of the dreamer?

2. Jeans is by no means the only scientist to ask questions such as this which express a profound spiritual suspicion or expectation when considering science's surprising insights and surprises. The physicist Werner Heisenberg, one of the founders of quantum mechanics, wrote of "the almost frightening simplicity and wholeness of the relationships which nature suddenly spreads out before us." Erwin Schrodinger once commented that

> The world is big and great and beautiful. My scientific knowledge of the events in it comprises hundred of millions of years. Yet in another way it is ostensibly contained in a poor seventy or eighty or ninety years granted to me—a tiny spot in immeasurable time, nay even in the finite millions and milliards of years that I have learnt to measure and assess. Whence come I and whither go I? That is the great unfathomable question, the same for every one of us. Science has no answer to it.

3. Albert Einstein too was inspired scientifically by a deep sense of mathematical beauty in the depths of nature. Like Schrodinger, he freely acknowledged the limits of science. He conceded that our efforts to understand the world and our place within it are but fumbling beginnings. He also celebrated "the logical simplicity of the order and harmony which we can grasp humbly and only imperfectly." Einstein described his sense of what he called a "cosmic religious feeling" as follows:

> The individual feels the futility of human desires and aims and the sublimity and marvelous order which reveal themselves both in nature and in the world of thought. . . . In my view, it is the most important function of art and science to awaken this feeling and keep it alive in those who are receptive to it.

4. Many scientists who are not religious in the conventional sense nevertheless have a deep sense of awe and respect for the majesty of the universe and celebrate the felicitous and ingenious order in nature. Stephen Hawking, whose famous book *A Brief History of Time* is often mistakenly interpreted as an attack on religion, remarks:

> Ever since the dawn of civilization, people have not been content to see events as unconnected and inexplicable. They have craved an understanding of the underlying order in the world. Today we still yearn to know why we are here and where we came from. Humanity's deepest desire for knowledge is justification enough for our continuing quest.

5. For those many scientists who now believe in creative divinity the feeling that scientific inquiry opens a special door on divine handiwork is irresistible. Dr. Allan Sandage, former director of Mount Wilson Observatory, said:

> The world is incredible—just the fact that you and I are here, that the atoms of our bodies were once part of stars. They said I am on

some kind of religious quest, looking for god, but god is the way it's put together. God is Newton's and Einstein's Laws.

6. Sandage is not alone in seeing divinity in the workings of the physical universe. Other scientists accompany him. In his highly acclaimed introduction to Einstein, Lincoln Barnett wrote in 1957:

> In the evolution of scientific thought, one fact has become impressively clear: there is no mystery of the physical world which does not point to a mystery beyond itself. . . . Man's inescapable impasse is that he himself is part of the world he seeks to explore; his body and proud brain are mosaics of the same elemental particles that compose the dark drifting clouds of interstellar space; he is, in the final analysis, merely an ephemeral conformation of the primordial space-time field. Standing midway between macrocosm and microcosm, he finds barriers on every side and can perhaps but marvel, as St. Paul did nineteen hundred years ago, that the world was created by the word of God so that what is seen was made out of things which do not appear.[15]

7. The famous Cambridge astronomer Sir Arthur Eddington tried to unite quantum physics and relativity with what he called his own mysticism, "his conviction that the universe worth studying is the one within us." He suggested that man should use "the higher faculties of his nature, so that they are no longer blind alleys but open out into a spiritual world—a world partly of illusion, no doubt, but in which he lives no less in the world, also of illusion, revealed by the senses."

8. Eddington wrote a parable about the small-minded egotism of a marine biologist who cast his net into the sea to accumulate a mass of evidence of what dwells in the deep. From the fish in his net, he arrived at two conclusions. First, no creature is less than two inches long; and secondly, all sea creatures have gills. A critic objected that the sea contained many creatures less than two inches long, but the scientist

would have to use a finer net if he wished to catch them. The scornful biologist replied, "anything uncatchable in my net is by that very fact outside the scope of fish science. What my net can't catch isn't a fish!"

9. Robert Boyd, a professor of physics at London University, has said,

> I think it is quite common to find Christians among scientists as in any other profession. In fact, I would say that, if anything, it is a little more common to find Christians among physicists than it is in some other branches of science.

10. Some astronomers at work discovering the vast complexities of the macrocosm, and nuclear physicists investigating the awesome variety of the microcosm, are concluding that the universe bears the hallmarks of intelligent design. Thus Jeans wrote that "the universe is beginning to look not so much like a great machine but like a great thought."

11. In their own ways, many scientists are reaffirming St. Paul's view that "Our eyes are fixed, not on things that are seen, but on the things that are unseen: for what is seen passes away; what is unseen is eternal" (2 Corinthians 4:18 NEB). Or as Henry Drummond wrote:

> The physical properties of spiritual matter form the alphabet which is put into our hands by God, the study of which, if properly conducted, will enable us more perfectly to read that great book which we call the Universe. . . . Law is great not because the phenomenal world is great, but because these vanishing lines are the avenues into the Eternal Order.[16]

12. St. Paul would have concurred with Drummond that "the visible is the ladder up to the invisible: the temporal is but the scaffolding of the eternal."

13. Ralph Waldo Trine wrote:

> Everything exists in the unseen before it is manifested or realized in the seen, and in this sense it is true that the unseen things are the

real, while the things that are seen are the unreal. The unseen things are cause; the seen things are the effect. The unseen things are the eternal and the seen things are the changing, the transient.[17]

14. On a cloudy day there appears to be no sun, but we have faith that it is only hidden. However, if we were to imagine a race of beings who had arisen on Venus, which is always totally covered by thick clouds, we could see that many of them might be "agnostics," who might never be comfortable with notions like a distant sun and stars and galaxies.

15. Modern physics provides useful examples of entities which are not directly available to observation. In quantum field theory, for instance, the forces between material particles are attributed to the exchange of invisible so-called virtual particles, or quanta. Although these virtual particles cannot be directly detected, they leave an imprint on the world of tangible things through their subtle interactions. Even a vacuum—apparently empty space—is teeming with virtual quanta of many varieties, the presence of which causes tiny but measurable disturbances to the energy levels of atoms.

16. Lowell Fillmore wrote in 1963, "Until we tune in our mind to perceive god's kingdom, we judge the world by appearances only, and therefore behold only the dark things in the world."

17. Our five senses provide us with the capacity to perceive only a few of the myriad notes in the complex and intricate creative symphony of life which surrounds us. The unknown appears to extend vastly beyond the area of the known. Can human concepts and evidences of the spiritual unknown increase over 100 fold in the 21st century? By spending 1% of income on science research, information about visible things did increase over 100 fold in the 20th century alone.

18. Astronomers have estimated that the gravitating mass in the universe is roughly ten times greater than can be accounted for by vis-

ible stars and galaxies. Some guess that the substantial discrepancy is caused by black holes. Others have proposed thin gas between galaxies. In all, there are over thirty suggested forms of dark or invisible objects that might make up this unseen ocean of cosmic matter. Theoretical physicists have even speculated that, in addition to normal matter, there may be a type of shadow matter, particles such as electrons and protons, identical to those we are made of but interacting with normal matter only via gravitation. Such shadow matter could exist all around us. We would notice it only from its gravitational pull, the weakest of nature's forces. Hypothetically, there could even exist shadow beings occupying the same time and space as we do that would go entirely unnoticed because our world and the world of unseen reality are so feebly coupled.

19. By reading the following long list of illustrations of exploring concepts, which Professor Paul Davies wrote in 1998, can we learn to be more humble about how little we yet know, including possibilities for researches to discover vastly more about the creator and his purposes?

a) Central to the humble approach is the acknowledgment that the world as revealed to our senses is but an infinitesimal fraction of all that exists. The power of science augments and extends those senses, but even as scientists open up new vistas with their instruments, so they discover that there may be yet more to the universe—perhaps vastly more—than we ever imagined. The more they find, the more they find there is to find. Our knowledge is like an island in a vast ocean of the unknown. The larger the island becomes, the larger is the boundary with the unknown.

b) When Hubble made his famous observations that led to the discovery of the expanding universe, he was able to compute the farthest distance that telescopes could in principle probe. This distance, called the particle horizon, is defined as the limit beyond which no galaxies (or particles) can be seen because they would effectively be retreating from us faster than the speed of light. The answer was several billion light years. To put this in perspective light takes only eight and a half minutes to cross the ninety six million miles from the sun to the earth. In one year it travels six trillion miles. A universe several billion light years in size is beyond all human imagining.

c) Vast though the cosmos of the astronomers may be, scientists increasingly question whether Hubble's universe is itself just a tiny "bubble" of space in a much larger—possibly infinite—assemblage of spatial regions, sometimes dubbed "the multiverse." Cosmologists have been led to this remarkable concept by trying to understand the physics of the very early universe, the hot dense phase that came immediately after the big bang. The four basic forces of nature are believed to be four facets of an underlying superforce. As the energy of interaction is raised, so the forces successively merge together in identity. Thus, at a hundred thousand times typical nuclear energies, the electromagnetic and weak nuclear forces are observed to become one single "electroweak" force. Theoretical physicists using mathematical models suspect that at an energy some ten trillion times greater still, the strong nuclear force would merge with the electroweak force, while at ten thousand times this enormous energy, gravitation would also join in, forming a solitary master force.

d) It is likely that energies of this magnitude have not been achieved anywhere in the observable universe since the first moments after the big bang. At that time matter was so hot and so compressed that, for the briefest duration, the super-force reigned supreme. As the universe cooled from that flash of primeval heat, so the four forces successively "crystallized out." And along with the forces of nature, the various familiar particles were created from the immense reserves of heat energy. The crystallization of the forces and particles can be compared to the domains of a magnet. A normal iron bar magnet is made up of lots of tiny magnetic domains that are aligned to produce an ordered pattern. When iron is heated above the so-called Curie point, it loses its magnetization because the different domains swivel about with random orientations, and their magnetic fields average to zero. As the iron cools, so the domains freeze their motions, and the magnetization is able to reappear. However, if there is no externally imposed magnetic field, the different domains may orient themselves differently, with no overall preference for one direction or another. In the same way, following the big bang, the fundamental forces and particles might "freeze" differently in different regions of space. There could be other domains of the universe, far beyond range of the most powerful telescopes, in which the forces and particles are different. These differences could be one of degree—the relative strengths of the forces might be unlike their values in our region—or one of form—there may be five forces instead of four, for example.

e) Some physicists have conjectured that in addition to the three dimensions of space and one of time that we observe in daily life, there could be additional dimensions of space that go unseen because they are "rolled up" to a very small size. To take an analogy, imagine viewing a hosepipe from afar; it appears like a wiggly line. On closer inspection however, the line turns out to be a tube, and each point on the line is really a little circle going around the tube. Likewise, what we think is a point of three-dimensional space might in reality be a little circle going around a fourth dimension. There is no limit to the number of extra dimensions that can be concealed in this way. In the fashionable string theory, there are six extra dimensions, rolled up to a size twenty powers of ten smaller than an atomic nucleus. According to the theory, when the universe originated in the big bang, all nine space dimensions were on a par, but as the universe cooled, so three dimensions expanded to cosmological size, while the other six remained curled up. This raises the question of why three dimensions were chosen to behave differently from the rest. Perhaps it was only chance that selected three, just as chance determines the orientation of a particular domain of a magnet. If so, then other domains of the universe may have different numbers of dimensions. Just what the physical properties would be like in a universe with different forces, different particles and different numbers of dimensions can only be guessed at. Yet it is entirely possible that in the totality of the multiverse, our "Hubble bubble" is just one of an infinite variety of bubbles of expanding space in which all manner of physical laws might be manifested.

f) An alternative type of domain structure has been suggested by the physicist Andre Linde, based on the inflationary universe scenario. In the original form of this scenario, proposed in the early 1980s by Alan Guth, shortly after the big bang the universe suddenly jumped in size by an enormous factor—at least forty powers of ten. This violent inflation lasted only a trillion trillion trillionth of a second before giving way to the normal, slower rate of expansion. Nevertheless, in the fleeting duration that inflation persisted, a region of space the size of an atom would have expanded to at least the size of a football. In Linde's variant of the scenario, exceedingly rapid inflation continued in some regions of space and ceased in others. As a result, on a very large scale space is still expanding at breakneck speed, but distributed within this infinite volume are "bubbles" of space like our own, billions of light years across, expanding much more slowly. Each individual bubble may have a cycle of birth, expansion and perhaps death in a "big crunch," but on the larger scale, in the multiverse as a whole, there is eternal renewal as new bubble universes are continually being born at random points in the inflating space.

g) Yet another variant on this theme has been proposed by Alan Guth and developed by physicist Lee Smolin, drawing upon earlier ideas of John Wheeler. This theory is based on the mystery of what happens to a star that collapses to form a black hole. One possibility is that the region of space within the hole balloons out to form an entirely new universe. From outside the black hole, the region of space looks very compact—perhaps only a few kilometers across—but for an observer inside the hole, the situation resembles the big bang. In effect, a new universe is born within the hole, creating its own space as it expands. This universe may in turn form black holes and give rise to yet more universes and so on, *ad infinitum*. Smolin conjectures that the laws of physics may be "reprocessed" during the violence of the gravitational collapse, so that the new universe may emerge with different physical properties. Once again, on the large scale of the multiverse, one has a picture of an assemblage of island universes, each enormous bubbles of space throughout which the physical laws are uniform but differing from one bubble to the next, thus bestowing upon the multiverse an almost limitless variety of possibilities and giving exuberant expression to the biblical concept of god's house of many mansions.

h) These various proposals for enlarging our view of the cosmos on an astronomical scale have been matched by equally intriguing and radical ideas from the micro-realm of quantum mechanics. Here the mystery is not what happens inside a black hole, but what turns the fuzzy and indeterminate world of quantum uncertainty into the concrete deterministic world of human observations.

i) In spite of its enormous success, the subject of quantum mechanics remains a profound riddle. Everyone agrees that the theory works brilliantly, but scientists are sharply divided over what the equations actually mean. The key issue concerns the nature of reality. Most scientific theories assume that there exists an independent real world and that the purpose of the theory is to explain how things are "out there." Quantum mechanics is different. It does not tell us how things *are* but only how they appear to an observer. It denies that we can ever make sense of an independent reality, because observer and observed are inextricably entangled in quantum phenomena.

j) Although this sounds rather mystical, it has very definite consequences. For example, Newton's theory of mechanics described the movement of material bodies under the action of forces. It makes perfect sense to ask, say, where a planet might be located in its orbit around the sun today. By contrast, if you ask where an electron is located at some moment in its orbit around an atomic nucleus, the theory tells you that the question is meaningless. It denies the very existence of well-defined paths in space for atoms and subatomic particles. Although an electron is a point-like particle, its movement cannot be pinned down moment by moment with precision.

k) This fuzziness in the behavior of electrons and all subatomic particles is the basis of the famous uncertainty principle of Werner Heisenberg. Roughly speaking, it says that a particle cannot have definite values of both position and momentum at the same time. You can measure the position of an electron and obtain a definite value, but then its motion will be completely uncertain. Alternatively, you can measure how it moves, but then you lose all knowledge of its position. It is meaningless to ask what the electron is really doing, for quantum mechanics says that the uncertainty is inherent in nature itself. Even the electron doesn't know where it is and how it is moving.

l) One consequence of quantum uncertainty is that events in the microcosm cannot be predicted in detail. Fire an electron at a target and it may bounce to the left. Repeat the experiment with identical circumstances and next time it might bounce to the right. We may give the betting odds for one or the other outcome but not an accurate prediction on a case-by-case basis. Quantum mechanics is therefore a fundamentally statistical theory that describes an indeterminate world, a view that Albert Einstein could never accept. "God does not play dice with the universe," he declared.

m) Unfortunately for Einstein, it seems that the processes of nature are indeed a game of chance at the microscopic level. The fate of an electron or other subatomic particle generally cannot be decided in advance. This raises a very deep question about reality. Consider the experiment where an electron is fired at a target. Suppose the experimenter chooses not to look whether it bounced to the left or the right. What can then be said about the electron after it has hit the target? It is tempting to believe that the electron is really moving either to the left or right, even if we do not know which. However, the rules of quantum mechanics forbid that conclusion. Rather, we must suppose that in some sense the electron is following *both* routes!

n) One way to think about this paradoxical situation is to imagine two possible worlds, one with a left-moving electron, the other with a right-moving electron. If no observation is made, then both worlds must be considered to co-exist. It is rather like projecting two movies onto the same screen. Quantum mechanics therefore describes ghostly overlapping realities—or at least potential realities. In the general case there will be not just two, but an infinity of alternative worlds present together. According to the rules of quantum mechanics as originally articulated by Niels Bohr in the 1930s, only when an observation is made does this ghostly superposition of alternative worlds get projected into a single, concrete reality.

o) Many of the founders of quantum mechanics recoiled from this strange view of nature. They tried to point up its absurdity by imagining experiments that would bring out its paradoxical aspects in a stark and dramatic way. Perhaps the most famous of these thought experiments is the cat paradox of Erwin Schrödinger. It was designed to illustrate the weirdness of the quantum world by amplifying it from atomic dimensions up to an everyday scale. Imagine, said Schrödinger, that a cat was confined in a box with a flask of cyanide, some radioactive substance and a hammer poised above the flask, attached to a delicate mechanical device that would let the hammer fall if it detected the decay of a single radioactive atom. Suppose that after one minute there was a 50% chance that an atom had decayed, triggered the hammer, and killed the cat. If the experimenter then opens the box, there is a probability of one-half that the cat will be dead. But what could one say about the cat if no observation were made? As the contents of the box are made of atoms and are therefore subject to quantum principles, the theory says that after one minute the cat should be in a superposition of live and dead states. In other words, the cat is neither in a live nor a dead state but in some bizarre way an amalgam of the two! But surely, asked Schrödinger, the *cat* will know whether it is alive or dead? Therefore, something must be wrong with the reasoning.

p) Exactly what is wrong has been the subject of heated debate for over half a century. One increasingly popular resolution of the cat paradox is the many-worlds interpretation of quantum mechanics. According to this view, the two alternative realities—a world with a live cat and another with a dead cat—are both equally real and represent parallel universes. Each universe may have observers who think that their world is unique, for each observer sees only one reality, either a live cat or a dead cat—never both together. Of course, once the principle of multiple realities is conceded, then it is a small step to accept that there must be an infinity of parallel universes created by countless quantum processes going on throughout the cosmos.

q) The many-universes interpretation of quantum mechanics is by no means universally accepted by physicists, although some notable scientists have expressed their preference for it. If the theory is taken seriously, it means that the world of our experience is only one among an infinity of parallel universes. David Deutsch, one of the founders of the modern variant of the many-universes theory, has written:

> It follows that reality is much bigger than it seems—and most of it cannot be directly perceived. The part we call the universe—all the objects and events that we and our instruments can directly observe—is the merest tip of the iceberg.

r) The other ghost, or shadow, universes cannot be reached by traveling through space, however far one were to go. Instead, each has its own space and time. The relationship between the many universes is rather like the pages of a book, each page representing an entire universe of space, time, matter and—perhaps—observers. And just as the pages can be close to each other in a certain sense, even if separate, so too are there other universes in some sense very close to ours. Indeed, according to the rules of quantum mechanics, at the atomic level there can be "cross-over" and return, ensuring that ghostly influences will pass from one universe to another. These influences show up as so-called quantum coherence effects—effects that indirectly lead to observable phenomena, such as interference patterns and tiny forces between atoms.

The melding of alternate realities in the atomic realm is being put to practical use in a number of laboratories seeking to build quantum computers. A conventional computer is limited in the speed with which it can tackle certain complex calculations. One way of speeding things up is to use parallel processing, where different parts of the calculations are done simultaneously in different regions of the machine, and the results combined. In spite of this, some calculations are effectively intractable, because they would take even a supercomputer longer than the lifetime of the universe to reach an answer. One classic example is the factoring of very large numbers into primes, which is the basis of many military and commercial codes. A 150-digit number would take a supercomputer millions of years to factorize. A quantum computer, however, could perform the same task with an exponential improvement in speed and make all codes based on factorization vulnerable to rapid cracking. The reason for this is that a quantum computer would operate at the atomic level, performing switching operations in systems subject to quantum mechanical principles. Viewed in the many-universe picture, a quantum switch would be able to link many different universes, thus hooking the parallel worlds into the calculation. In effect, the quantum computer would use parallel processing not by exploiting other parts of the machine, but by exploiting other worlds! The computation could be carried out on a potentially infinite number of copies of the computer located in an infinite number of universes, and the results combined to obtain the output. Theorists have proved that many otherwise intractable problems could be solved in quick time by a quantum computer.

s) The existence of multiple quantum realities would never have been guessed by scientists a hundred years ago; in 2000 they are routinely discussed by physicists and are even the subject of government research grants. The radical revision of reality triggered by the quantum revolution is thus as profound as any in the history of mankind, and yet who is to say that it is the last word? What new concepts may emerge and what new discoveries might be made in the 21st century that would transform our picture of the universe equally radically? Even with the image of an infinity of parallel quantum worlds and a multiverse of infinitely varied bubbles, we may still be glimpsing only a tiny part of god's complexity and totality and only a tiny part of the ultimate universal reality.

20. These concepts in cosmology and biology listed by Professor Paul Davies could not have been predicted as recently as 1900, which is some reason to understand how difficult it can be in the year 2000 to predict clearly how spiritual information might increase over 100 fold in the next century, partly by future rigorous research not yet planned.

21. It may be useful to consider the ways in which we ourselves are a manifestation of this astonishing cosmos. What we think of as our selves (or young souls?) seems to be something we own that is separate and ours. Yet can selves be temporary manifestations of patterning of a much greater and vaster reality which makes our earthly education possible and sustains it?

22. Should we note that the physical body from which our sense of self (or soul) "emerges" may be a dynamic object rather than a strictly material one? The composition of our body is constantly changing as new material enters it and replaces in a never-ending process the material constituents we are made of. The nature of the conscious mind which arises from within us is itself like a kind of immaterial field of complex interaction based on a constant infeed of metabolic energy. In one sense it is a non-material evanescence, but in another, it is the center of command. But if we were to try in any sense to weigh the property of the conscious mind, it would represent a vanishingly miniscule addition of mass based on its energy content converted to mass via the well-known equation $E=mc^2$.

23. Should our bodies also be thought of as a process-in-flux—essentially a complex symbiotic colony of cells which has continuity only through very careful controls on temperature and the flow in and out of oxygen, carbon dioxide, water, nutrients, salts, iron, calcium and a wide range of other trace mineral constituents? Our distinctiveness as individual selves is composed of many tiny and seemingly nonmaterial evanescent things: with the specifics of complex collections of microscopic information strings (genes) which code for protein synthesis in our cells, and with a wide variety of aspects of the "wired-in" neural structuring in our brains, including its complex chemical balance and the content of memories and aspects of emotional responses. Tiny quantities of neuroactive chemicals can put a stop to the process that generates our selves, either permanently—as in the case of cobra venom—or temporarily—as in the case of nitrous oxide laughing gas. Key points to ponder are two. First, while we often feel that we are the "lords and masters" of our reality, in fact, is it only by the most evanescent physical links that we can exist at all? Second, does our existence as selves (or young souls) arise only out of the deep and astonishing symphony of underlying reality which provides the music which the physicists have pursued in their many and astonishing discoveries?

24. Would it be narrow and egotistical to think that nothing exists in the universe except what these cell colonies called humans have yet learned to touch or see? Would this be like a worm denying the existence of a butterfly because of its lack of eyesight, or a stone denying its dimensions and weight because it cannot comprehend arithmetic? Is it, after all, without purpose that human beings access the world through a limited range of senses and a narrow filter of mental imagery?

25. Is a tree a manifestation of god? In a greater sense, are humans a manifestation? Likewise, the sense evidence used in observational science may also be a manifestation of the spiritual world, but only a small

part. The seen and the unseen both exist together; but the seen is limited and temporary.

26. Emanuel Swedenborg was a religious thinker of the 18th century deeply influenced by the discoveries of Newton but eager to demonstrate that they had potential for a lived "spiritual" context. Newton had described space, famously, as the "sensorium" of god. Swedenborg developed his ideas with a more specifically panentheistic tendency. He taught that nothing exists separate from god. If god is infinite and includes the entire cosmos, then how can anything be separate from him? As St. Paul remarked to the Athenians, quoting a Hellenistic poet (Acts 17:28), "In him we live and move and have our being." Swedenborg claimed, god is all of you and you are a little part of god. Swedenborg taught that realization of this link between the visible world and the underlying and greater reality of divinity was vital. Also, that man is not in heaven until heaven is in man. Swedenborg believed that life had the potential to engage in a realization of the underlying linkage between people and divinity—a kind of "divinization." He taught that on this material earth we may begin to receive the life and spirit of heaven within us. We are citizens of the spiritual world, and maybe we are spirits (souls) from the day of our first breath. Love, loyalty, patience and mercy are more real than are tangible objects. God seeks to instill these spiritual realities into our own lives here and now. Taking the humble approach one also can see this material world as perhaps an incubator, provided by god, in which our spirits can develop and seek their ultimate expression in a realm invisible to us.

27. Edwin A. Abbot was an English clergyman, schoolmaster and amateur mathematician who in 1882 wrote a delightful and humorous fantasy called *Flatland*. The purpose of the book was to demonstrate the limited ability of the human mind to comprehend the possible existence of a greater reality around us. The people of Flatland lived in

only two dimensions. They denied the possibility of any being of three dimensions. Yet objects of three dimensions produced miraculous and mysterious phenomena by moving into or out of Flatland. The hero of the story, Mr. Square, visited the land of no dimension (Spotland) and the land of one dimension (Lineland) whose inhabitants refused to believe in the existence of any creature of two dimensions. After returning from his later visit to the wondrous land of three dimensions (Spaceland), his Flatland rulers put him in prison for life lest he should stir up trouble among Flatlanders by talk of realms which transcend two dimensions. Finally, Mr. Square says, "I will endure this and worse, if by any means I may arouse in the interiors of Planes and Solid Humanity a spirit of rebellion against the conceit which would limit our dimensions to two or three or any number short of infinity." Mr. Square begs his readers not to suppose that every minute detail in the daily life of Flatland must correspond to some other detail in Spaceland; and yet he hopes that, taken as a whole, his work may prove suggestive as well as amusing to those Spacelanders of moderate and modest minds, who, speaking of that which is of the highest importance but lies beyond experience, decline to say on the one hand, "This can never be," and on the other hand, "It must needs be precisely thus, and we know all about it."

28. Like the two-dimensional inhabitants of Flatland who formed their two-dimensional concepts of what can exist, many skeptics fail to account for limits on perception in debates over the existence of god. The philosophical issue of the existence of the world "within" god has been discussed in various ways. Some have argued that god is our "ultimate end" or the "ground of being" or "original cause" or the "power" that maintains our existence. The basis of considering such concepts, either favorably or critically, perhaps can best be approached with an appropriate humility. Humility recognizes the smallness of

human perception and logic and expects few answers but rather discovery of more mysteries.

29. Some think that supernatural events, such as miracles, are needed to prove god's existence. But is not the entire world we see daily a miracle in itself? It seems straightforward that if the world is a divine creation, then its natural processes are likely to be effective in accomplishing continuing creative purposes over whatever time scale and through whatever means. Thus, when new laws and more galaxies are discovered by human scientists, do they not merely discover a little more of god's activity and infinity? Certainly several of the most prominent amongst the early modern scientists believed in a view of nature as in some sense "the hand of god." Galileo, Newton, Descartes, Kepler and most of their colleagues were deeply religious. They thought that god had made the world and ordered it according to certain fixed laws. These scientists thought that, through their science, they were lifting a veil on divine handiwork, enabling them to glimpse the mind of god, albeit in an imperfect and limited way. For them, science was not the enemy of religion but a complement to worship and to spiritual discovery, another means to behold wonderful divine creation.

30. Each of us every day is swimming in an ocean of unseen miracles. For example, as we have seen, is it not unreasonable to view each living cell as a miracle; and the human body is a vast colony of over a hundred billion cells? The human brain consisting of three hundred billion neurons forms a network of interconnections of staggering complexity. In this vast community of brain interconnection, dubbed an "enchanted loom" by the physiologist Sir Arthur Sherrington, indescribably complex patterns of chemo-electrical activity interact, giving rise to the yet-to-be-explained phenomenon of consciousness: a miracle made of miracles! Does the miracle of this body and mind include both

our ability to recognize it as well as our inability ever to exhaust the true significance of it? As Einstein noted, "The most incomprehensible thing about the universe is that it is comprehensible." That the universe exhibits order, more than chaos, suggests the futility of trying to fathom the nature of matter without also investigating the unseen spirit.

31. Each time new laws are discovered by scientists, we potentially can learn a little more about divinity. William Jennings Bryan once answered the famous atheist Ralph Ingersoll on this point of recognizing the unseen in the seen. One day, Ingersoll saw an attractive globe of the earth in Bryan's office. He asked, "Who made it?" Bryan replied, "No one. It just made itself." While the discoveries of the nature and processes of biological evolution clearly have challenged traditional notions of natural teleology, especially in the context of theological determinism, they have not in any clear sense determined that the natural order is a purposeless accident. Aspects of purpose emerge within nature, from the most simple one-cell organism responding to external stimuli and maintaining homeostasis, to the human animal who plans long-range goals and contemplates life's ultimate purpose. It seems as if the evolutionary process rewards emergence of the capability of purposefulness as an adaptive advantage. Can this, and the vast, complex and sublime order of mathematical physics which undergirds it, be a mistake? Would it not be strange if a universe without purpose accidentally created humans who are so obsessed with purpose?

32. The extent to which spirit and matter, the unseen and the seen, are related has been hotly debated over the centuries by theists, atheists, agnostics, pantheists, panentheists and others. The fact that these arguments continue suggests that this is still a lively question among thinking people. While the concept of purpose in a cosmological and ontological sense applied to biology remains to be developed in clear scientific sense, some aspects of nature which act in a broad direction generating what

might be called "creative complexification" are clearly observed. Unseen properties of the world seem to provide its main features. Thus, even in biology, the vast unseen has not lost its power to tantalize our imaginations and inspire worship.

33. Traditionally, Christian theologians have conceived god as both immanent and transcendent—within the universe at all places and times, but also beyond and above it. Often the transcendence was emphasized, giving god a remoteness and detachment that made divinity appear utterly differentiated from his creations and sometimes as quite detached from them. Some recent philosophers and theologians reject the idea that two separate realities dwell together in one creature and have concluded that nothing can exist in separation from god. Paul Tillich, a Christian theologian, referred to god as the "ground of being." But Mary Baker Eddy, Charles Fillmore and Ernest Holmes have suggested that matter may be only an outward manifestation of divine thought. According to such thinking, the creative spirit called god may be the only reality.

34. The humble approach asks whether divinity is limitless and timeless, while created objects are contingent and temporary and finite. Does even the vast visible universe fall infinitely short of what god is? Is divinity continually creating each object and person and the cosmic universes? For thousands of years men and women were so short-sighted and self-centered that they thought the universe was not much larger than the earth. With more humility and knowledge, we now think the universe is a billion, billion, billion times more vast. Do we thus conceive of divine infinity as a higher degree of conceptual surprisingness (if we may coin a phrase) than we had previously supposed?

35. Can excitement and enthusiasm for the scientific study of nature and the cosmos be enhanced (not reduced) if we conceive of each discovery as being essentially a new revelation of divine reality?

36. When discoveries point more to the insubstantial nature of matter, does it become easier to think of matter and spirit as a unity? Einstein's theory of relativity makes it easier to understand that space and time may not be exactly what they appear to be to our everyday perception. Quantum mechanics in similar ways also reveals that the nature of reality is far more subtle than common sense might suggest. Can't these and many more discoveries cause us to be increasingly humble about saying that what we see is real and what we do not see is illusion? Such observations suggest that people who affirm a spiritual concept of life should not feel that science has shown their point of view to be unrealistic. Perhaps such people may agree with Lowell Fillmore, that they can "remember that although god's principles are spirit and cannot be seen, they are more real than tangible things. God's principles are fundamental and infinitely more far-reaching than the principles of mathematics and physics. His invisible principles uphold that which is visible to us." Or, as it is stated in the letter to the Hebrews, "By faith we understand that the world was created by the word of God, so that what is seen is made out of things which do not appear" (Hebrews 11:3 RSV).

37. Traditional pantheism can serve a useful purpose in suggesting the co-terminacy of spirit and matter and a personal relationship between the creator and creation. But it may not be compatible with the Christian concept of a personal god vastly greater than material things and who loves all of us and numbers the hairs of our heads. Profound mutual indwelling between man and divinity may be better stated by the Unity School of Christianity, "God is all of me: and I am a little part of him." Such a notion implies an inseparable relationship between god and us. As even "a little part of him," we may realize the mutual unity of god and his creation. We may conceive that our own divinity may arise from something more profound than merely being "god's children" or being "made in his image."

38. The atheist rests certain in belief that the physical universe is all that exists, and that it exists in a fundamental sense reasonlessly. The magnificent edifice of scientific discovery pointing to a lawfulness, order and harmony of the cosmos are blindly accepted as given. Atheism appeals to the rational order of the cosmos as an explanation for natural phenomena. However, it has difficulty in seeking explanations for that rational order itself if it appears this might merely open up more mystery and limited explanatory possibility rather than a full and coherent self-contained explanation.

39. Like Thoreau, humble people hope that some ponds will always be thought of as bottomless so that the concepts of the infinite and the unseen and the unfathomable can be part of our daily experience.

40. Increasingly, recent research indicates that health of the body can often be improved not only by chemicals but also by mind and spirituality. Recent studies around the world reveal the close interaction of body, mind and spirit in the healing process. More and more doctors are talking about healing the patient in addition to curing the disease. Often the latter may be achieved by chemistry and physical therapy. The former, however, also needs psychological and spiritual remedies not always available to the health care delivery team. Recent research by medical doctors yields increasing evidence that total health is not reducible to material explanations alone.

41. Those taking the humble approach think that the whole universe and all the creatures within it, both visible and invisible, may come from the eternal divinity and may be manifestations of god's infinite creative power. All of nature reveals something of the creator. And god is revealing himself more and more to human inquiry, not always through prophetic visions or scriptures but through the astonishingly productive research of modern scientists. In a way, the advance of modern scientific

understanding might be thought of as a golden age as god reveals many aspects of his creative intentionality and brilliance to human minds. How much more true today is the affirmation St. Paul wrote so long ago:

> For what can be known about God is plain to them, because God has shown it to them. Ever since the creation of the world his invisible nature, namely, his eternal power and deity, has been clearly perceived in the things that have been made (Romans 1:19–20 RSV).

42. In the 17th century, the poet John Milton phrased it, "What if earth be but the shadow of heaven, and things therein each to other like more than on earth is thought?"

43. Is the universe a home for love? Perhaps the answer depends not only on divine spirit but even on us. We transform ideas into action. But of all the aspects of the vast unseen, perhaps learning unselfish unlimited love most importantly requires diligent human work. Maybe the more we create, the more in some ways we are like god or serve as his helpers. We may especially reflect god if we create out of love.

44. Thus, in the end, humility raises the morally challenging question of whether possibly the purpose of humans is to become helpers in the accelerating creativity expressed in the famous equation in theology, "God is love."

CHAPTER SEVEN

Progressing Concepts
of the Mystery of Time

1. The nature of time occupies a central place in our understanding of the physical universe and our place within it. Many ancient cultures held that the universe is cyclic, with no beginning or end. Time was thus identified with periodic rhythms, somewhat like the rhythms of yearly seasons, with renewal and rebirth interspersed with aging and decay. Such cosmic cyclicity was taught by Plato and other Greek philosophers. It remains a fundamental part of much Hindu and Buddhist religion, and elements of it can also be found in music, art and literature in all contemporary cultures. The myth of the eternal return, as it has been called by anthropologist Mircea Elaide, pervaded religious practice and ritual among some very ancient peoples worldwide. Yearly rhythms and honors in the modern world in Christian countries are remembered in the celebration of annual festivals, especially new year and midsummer.

2. In contrast to the cyclic worldview is that of linear time—time represented symbolically as a straight line rather than a circle. Linear time is often described as a Western cultural creation, but it may be more accurate to identify it more broadly simply with monotheism. It appears first with Judaism and the notion that the history of the universe forms an unfolding progression, a cosmic story with a beginning, a middle and an end. The Jews sought to understand god through his

action in history; and a historical narrative needs directionality rather than cyclicity. The universe is portrayed as a project—god's project for which mankind is co-opted—with definite goals and an end state as well. Judaism thus contains a genesis and an eschatology, a creation and a culmination.

3. A linear concept of time was incorporated within both Christianity and Islam as well. For most Christians the ordered sequence is creation, fall, incarnation, redemption, judgment and eternal fulfillment. Like the Jews, Christians and Muslims believed that god created the world at a definite moment in the past and imposed upon the world a lawlike order that persists. But although the laws, both physical and moral, may not change, the conditions of the world change from moment to moment. Thus there can be design, a way that things are. In this concept, the world is not arbitrary or capricious or incoherent but part of an all-embracing cosmic plan, a rational plan that human beings are intimately caught up in. It is a created world, the product of an intelligent designer.

4. Modern science emerged in Europe under the combined influence of Christian monotheism, Renaissance humanism and the impact of revived learning stimulated by the rediscovery of Greek philosophy. The Greek belief that the world is rational and comprehensible was preserved through the Dark Ages by Islam and reintroduced into Europe in medieval times. Combined with a long heritage of Christian theology as developed in thinkers such as Augustine and redeveloped by a rich variety of scholastic thinkers, including Aquinas, Scotus, and others, which ratified the notion of a created world and a linear time, the new perspective formed a potent mix that may have helped the rise of what we now would call the empirical scientific worldview. For example, Newton made linear time the basis of his theory of mechanics. The so-called clockwork universe associated with Newtonian mechan-

ics captures very well the concept of the universe as a linear timepiece, an elaborate mechanism marking the inexorable passage of time with mathematical precision. In the 19th century, the discovery of the laws of thermodynamics introduced more directionality into the workings of nature, a one-way trend from low to high entropy. Heat flows irreversibly from hot to cold bodies. Such processes impose upon nature an arrow of time that manifests itself in countless ways, but most obviously in the aging of human beings. Similarly, the concept of evolution of life by Charles Darwin further reinforced notions of temporal directionality. The discovery of modern notions of cosmological evolution and of the physical "arrow of time" have continued, changing ideas from cyclic to linear time.

5. The old worldviews, however much they differed from one another, had certain things in common. Typical were their constricted dimensions, mechanistic structure and static character. Their constricted dimensions—the Ptolemaic picture of things—continued in vogue for more than a thousand years, up to the time of Copernicus. In this historically accepted way of envisaging the cosmos, reality was seen as a globe encompassed by huge crystalline spheres. It was not until modern times that mankind become aware of the gigantic dimensions and enormous structure of the universe.

6. It took the uncovering of the laws of nature by science to reveal just how profound is the lawlike order in nature. Science leads to a more predictable view of the universe by revealing both its mathematical beauty, harmony and ingenuity, but also the subtle connections between disparate phenomena. By linking the fall of an apple with the motion of the moon, Newton opened the way to a unification of terrestrial and celestial phenomena and the concept of god's universal laws that could be discerned by human beings through a process of careful reasoning and observation.

7. Fierce debates accompanied these momentous conceptual developments, not the least of which concerned the relationship of god to time. Classical Christian theology, at least since the time of Augustine in the 5th century, has held that god is located outside of time altogether; he is the creator of time. "Thou hadst made time itself," wrote Augustine. "The world was made with time, not in time." Augustine's and Aquinas's god is portrayed as a perfect, unchanging, timeless being who seems also somewhat remote and detached from the temporal affairs of men and women.

8. The 20th century also witnessed great revolutions in the physicist's understanding of time, especially the development of Einstein's two theories of relativity. Einstein was able to show that time is not absolute and universal but relative to the state of motion of the observer. Thus two observers who move differently will measure different durations between the same pair of events. This remarkable fact has been amply confirmed by experiment and leads to the famous twins effect. In this scenario, twin A travels to a nearby star at close to the speed of light and then returns to earth to find that twin B has aged considerably more. On A's clock, the journey has taken two years, but on B's clock it may have taken ten years. In effect, A has traveled eight years into B's future! Experiments very clearly have shown that such a scenario is realizable, though impractical from a technological viewpoint.

9. In 1895, ten years before Einstein published his special theory of relativity in which he predicted the twins effect, H. G. Wells wrote *The Time Machine*. This novel deals with a theme that explorers have dreamed about for centuries—the ability to travel backward and forward in time as though it were like travel over the face of the earth. Until only a thousand years ago, the only way to travel backward in time was imaginatively through history, which led one back only six

thousand years. Then backward travel was extended by archaeology, paleontology and geology to about four billion years. In the 20th century, astronomers realized they could look backward into time through light signals traveling towards us from the past at 186,000 miles per second. Quasars, some of which are estimated at twelve billion light years distant, look as they did when the universe was young, because the light we see left them that long ago.

10. In 2000 we know that Wells was right about travel into the future. Although a dramatic demonstration of this effect would require movement at close to the speed of light—still a distant prospect given current technology—nevertheless time dilation can still be measured at modest speeds such as those of aircraft. Modern atomic clocks are so accurate that they can register the few billionths of a second discrepancy per hour differences between a clock in the plane and an identical clock remaining on the ground.

11. Though travel into the future is in 2000 (at least in very small ways) a demonstrated reality, the possibility of actually visiting the past rather than merely observing it by the delay in light waves from distant astronomical objects is far more conjectural. Nevertheless, it remains an open question being actively investigated by theoretical physicists. One idea is the so-called wormhole conjecture. A wormhole is a topological bridge in space-time, which if real would allow an observer to travel a short distance through and emerge at a very distant place in the universe. If such an entity were to exist, it could also serve as a time machine, enabling the observer who traverses the wormhole and returns to his starting point to get back before he left! This concept breaches causal logic because it generates paradoxes such as the possibility of making one's own birth impossible. Consequently, it is clear that the modern scientific concept of time remains a deep and vexing mystery. Although we understand the subtleties of time far more than

did our ancestors, it is still not known for certain what time is and whether it is truly basic or something that derives from a deeper level of reality.

12. By revealing that time and space are part of the physical universe, closely linked to matter and energy, Einstein's work reopened the debate about god's relationship to time. If god is thought to be the ultimate creator of the physical universe, and not to be subject to the principles of a preexisting natural order, then god must also be the creator of time, as Augustine had long ago insisted.

13. Einstein's theory of general relativity has been developed in terms of a wide variety of world models or mathematical universes. Some of these have provided a scientific context for understanding how time might have a definite origin at a finite moment in the past. The general theory of relativity describes gravitation as a warping or distortion in the geometry of space and time. It also predicts that if a configuration of matter becomes sufficiently compressed, nothing can prevent it from imploding without limit. Translated into geometry, this state of affairs corresponds to an infinite curvature of space-time, known to mathematicians as a singularity. Since neither space nor time can be continued smoothly through a point of infinite curvature, a singularity can be thought of as a boundary or edge to space-time.

14. In recent years there have been attempts to go beyond the orthodox theory in the hope of providing a more fully scientific account of the cosmic origin. Specially notable are works of James Hartle and Stephen Hawking. These two physicists applied the theory of quantum mechanics to the origin of the universe and made a curious discovery. Although Einstein showed that space and time are not independent but linked in a four dimensional space-time, nevertheless space is still space and time is still time. Quantum physics blurs even this distinction. According to Heisenberg's uncertainty principle, on a very small scale

of length and duration, it is possible for the identities of space and time to become somewhat merged and uncertain.

15. Hartle's and Hawking's work has been widely reported as an attack on god because, to use Hawking's own words, there is "nothing left for god to do." However, is this a simplistic misunderstanding of the nature of classical Christianity? If science may provide a satisfactory explanation of how the universe came into being from nothing, based on the existence of physical laws like those of quantum mechanics, does that change the need for a purposeful underpinning for all existence? Science may explain the origin of the universe, but what explains science? Where do the very laws to which Hawking and others appeal come from in the first place?

16. The ongoing creativity of nature has been recognized and celebrated in many theological works since 1800. A notable contribution was made by Alfred North Whitehead, the British mathematician and philosopher, who founded a school of thought known as process theology. Process thought stresses the intimate involvement of god in the unfolding of his creation at each moment. Do god and the universe form a mutually interacting whole, a sort of physical and spiritual unity, progressing continually and possibly accelerating?

17. Another influential thinker along these lines was the Jesuit mystic and respected paleontologist Teilhard de Chardin. He pointed out that in the long story of creation there came first development of a sphere of inanimate objects or mineral evolution, which he called the geosphere; then the sphere of living things, the biosphere; and lastly the sphere of the human mind, the "noosphere." This unexpected new world of the human mind is so potent and so novel that no one knows what may happen next. Is creativity accelerating? The evolution of ideas is of course many orders of magnitude more rapid than the evolution of the material cosmos. Is there any reason to think that this new

world of mind and free will must be the end of progress? Does the new vista massively amplify possibilities? What unexpected aspects of reality will emerge next? Will it be a new world of soul or spirit? Are we about to participate in a new dawn?

18. Given the ceaselessly creative nature of divinity and our universe, and the vast lengths of time available for life to emerge and evolve, it is only natural that we should speculate about the existence of intellects on other planets. The Nobel Prize-winning biologist Christian de Duve believes that the universe is "a hotbed of life." He writes:

> Life and mind emerge not as the results of freakish accidents, but as natural manifestations of matter, written into the fabric of the universe. I view this universe not as a "cosmic joke," but as a meaningful entity—made in such a way as to generate life and mind, bound to give birth to thinking beings able to discern truth, apprehend beauty, feel love, yearn after goodness, define evil, experience mystery.

19. The Milky Way galaxy consists of more than a hundred billion stars. There may be over a hundred billion other galaxies in the universe. If only one star in a thousand has planets, and if only one in a thousand of these has a planet resembling the earth, the arithmetic still indicates the possibility of ten million billion other earths in the visible universe. Some astronomers estimate that in our galaxy alone there may be millions of civilizations. Most scientists agree that *homo sapiens*, modern man, is not likely to be the end of creativity.

20. Most speculation about extraterrestrial intelligence assumes that it will be embodied in some form of flesh and blood, as on earth. However, would it be very egotistical to assume that the concept of mind (and soul) would be restricted in this way? Life may have the potentiality to exist in a multiplicity of different forms.

21. Has science gradually revealed evidence that all entities are continuously and intrinsically interconnected, so that we can now see the world as deeply interrelational in several aspects? Maybe an organic whole in which every single thing is related to everything else?

22. In overview we may recognize three principal characteristics of the modern view. These are: first, that we live in a universe gigantic in its dimensions; second, that probably life worlds within the cosmos are multiplying; and third, that this progress seems to be guided by a kind of law of complexification which has an accelerating tendency and which leads to new domains of creativity. Only after 1950 have we begun to study the expansion that this brings to human comprehension of divinity.

23. Naturally, new concepts of reality did not spring up overnight. Nor have these been the outcome of one particular branch of science. Small pockets of insight regarding the dynamic structure of things appeared here and there. Biology and its kindred life sciences have contributed even more than astronomy to forming new concepts, for it is from the study of forms of life that the idea of evolution, of a process of progressive and accelerating growth, is most clearly evident.

24. But, as students of the humble approach in both science and theology, we should pause to consider Sir Bernard Lovell's warning in 1978:

> The complex processes leading to our present understanding of the universe have led to a modern view of the cosmos which we believe to be substantially correct, but it will be a remarkable and indeed unique feature of human thought if this really is the case.[18]

25. Nevertheless, at this moment in time, scientists, theologians, laity, can all of us utilize this current worldview in our continuing participation in creation? Admitting we might be proven wrong by yet another conceptual framework better than what we presently understand, should we nonetheless launch forward in our scientific quest toward

new discoveries? And what new discoveries are to be made? Is evolution ending with humans on earth or only beginning? To think that humanity on this planet is the end of evolution would be egotistical and anthropocentric indeed. It has always been difficult to imagine what comes next, but does the multitude of discoveries in the 20th century of realities previously unseen point toward the likelihood of even more amazing discoveries hereafter?

26. Yet how astounding it is that after over 99% of the timespan of the evolution of the earth had taken place, a new creation, a new kind of creativity, could suddenly burst forth! The dramatic change was the appearance of humans, creatures with free will, the first on earth to be allowed to participate in the creative process. Until then, evolution seems to have followed a course fixed by laws of nature. But suddenly the inconceivable has happened: self-evolution, intentional creativity has begun. The earth is filled with creations of a new kind such as logic, love, mathematics, worship, purpose, inventions, and multitudes of other creations never seen on this planet before. After four billion years of earthly evolution a reality appeared, a world of mind and spirit.

27. Has human ingenuity helped to gain new understanding of the geosphere and biosphere? Synthetic materials begin to replace natural ones. In some parts of the world, inventions are rapidly creating standards of living and education never dreamed of by people before. Luther Burbank began to design and speed up the evolution of vegetables and flowers. Thousands of varieties which never existed before were invented by man to suit human needs and beautify nature. More than ever men and women are allowed to participate in the creation of a new world.

28. Do these new developments offer important opportunities for contemporary theology to enrich its domain and relevance? Humans now are faced with awesome technological possibilities for transformation of the human condition. These include intelligence enhancement,

lifespan extension and personality modification. Recently also, ways are being discovered to avoid the miseries which result from too many unwanted children, miseries for the pitiful children, the parents and their communities. Many people for good reason will find these prospects threatening. Indeed, it is clear that sometimes such abilities can be abused and cause great harm. Can such new abilities also accomplish extraordinary good? Theology, however, may not yet be equipped for this task. Thus, an exciting task of theology may be to envision worthy possibilities beyond current imagination and to help to cultivate a new theological vision sufficient to inspire researchers toward realizing such awesome possibilities in practical and beneficial ways. As St. Paul warned us:

> Things beyond our seeing, things beyond our hearing, things beyond our imagining, all prepared by God for those who love him, these it is that God has revealed to us through the Spirit. For the Spirit explores everything, even the depths of God's own nature. (1 Corinthians 2:9–10 NEB)

29. The 20th century after the time of Christ may very well have represented a new acceleration in human culture, a new embarkation into future cultures. Where can the creativity of modern science and technology take us if our vision is animated by a quest for following divine purposes? What are the possibilities most worth pursuing?

30. Does the present offer theology a greatly expanded vision of the cosmos and of historical process and potentiality? Most excitingly, is an important challenge for theology opened up on the possibility of spiritual progress? How can theologians and religious communities research ways to develop real and beneficial aspects of spiritual progress?

31. To answer these questions may require the development of close links between religious and scientific communities. The notion of spiritual progress is not yet very clearly defined, but there are many possibilities to be explored. To this topic we turn in the next chapter.

CHAPTER EIGHT

Possibilities for
Spiritual Progress?

1. Should we listen to the warning implied in the anthropological studies of Anthony Wallace, who claims that in the last hundred thousand years of human history, more than one hundred thousand different religions have flourished and disappeared? Wallace points out that this is surely evidence that in human nature there is always an abiding sense of god. But, is it also a clear indication that concepts of god that are too small do become obsolete and vanish? History is replete with little gods now forgotten. H. L. Menken compiled a list of over a hundred deities whose names now appear only in history books or as inscriptions on old monuments. Did belief in them die out because they were too rigidly or narrowly conceived and often associated with some tribal or national interests? Do concepts of divinity need to progress and evolve to keep pace with the growth of human knowledge and with continuing revelations of the universal creative spirit?

2. Often, we read the words *religious revival* or *renewal*. Great benefits come from reminding people of spiritual realities. Both are desirable, but are they enough? What would it mean if people spoke in this way about astronomy, physics, chemistry or medicine? Would "renewal of medical science" not sound a bit odd? Would the term "revival of chemistry" not imply a dying science in need of reviving?

Would chemistry be improved by a movement to restudy ideas in ancient books of alchemy? Is reviving the old enough to keep spiritual information in the vanguard of the knowledge explosion?

3. Can religious thought progress along with other aspects of the social, political, economic and scientific environment? If not, will people naturally grow dissatisfied? A *New York Times* study covering 1957 to 1970 chronicled Americans' replies to the question, "At the present time do you think religion as a whole is increasing its influence in American life or losing its influence?" The percentage who thought religion was indeed losing influence increased from 14% in 1957 to 75% in 1970. Reasons given for this decline in religious influence included statements that religion was "outdated" or "not relevant in today's world."[19] The Gallup organization has found even greater religious decline in Europe. Every nation in Europe has a lower church attendance percentage than America. In some nations still considered culturally to be Christian, church attendance by adults in 1999 fell below 10%. Such shrinkage appears in practically all the large, older Christian denominations. Also in the 20th century, the percentage of practicing Buddhists and Hindus in the world population has decreased.

4. Along with the decline in regular religious attendance at most of the older denominations, hundreds of new religious groups have formed especially since 1950, and many of them have grown like wildfire. When the 20th century began, for instance, there were no major denominations called pentecostal or charismatic. Yet, beginning without any formal organization, in dozens of nations more than a hundred new denominations of these kinds have sprung up, full of zeal and missionary outreach. In the United States alone, over fifty million people now describe themselves as born-again Christians. The first World Congress of Charismatics drew over fifty thousand delegates to Kansas City in 1977 from all over the world.

5. Television programs run by churches in the United States in 1999 draw audiences ten times greater than similar programs in 1960. At least a dozen church programs on television and radio claim audiences in the millions every week. More new church buildings are being erected than ever before. Circulation of church newspapers and magazines in the United States is breaking all-time records. In South Korea, the number of Christians increased eightfold from 1970 to 1998.

6. Young people are responding with enthusiasm to new interdenominational and international youth clubs and organizations. Youth for Christ, Young Life, InterVarsity, and Campus Crusade have become very influential.

7. With such revival in new religious interests and with the need to keep religion up-to-date and progressive, should churches and foundations now appropriate manpower and money for joint theological-scientific research? Should governments sponsor such impartial interfaith research just as they do science and cultural research? Because most natural scientists understand the scientific method better than do most theologians, should scientists undertake research projects independent of religious denominations and develop suitable methods of scientific inquiry into spiritual matters? Should people and foundations donate more for such research?

8. A variety of science and religion associations promoting constructive interaction between scientists and theologians and religious leaders have formed, including the Institute for Religion in an Age of Science (IRAS), the European Society of the Study of Science and Theology (ESSSAT), the American Scientific Affiliation (ASA), the Ian Ramsey Center, Christians in Science (CIS), the Society of Ordained Scientists (SOS), the Center for Theology and the Natural Sciences (CTNS), the Universite Interdisciplinaire de Paris (UIP), the Philadelphia Center for Religion and Science (PCRS), the Zygon

Center for Religion and Science (ZCRS), the Center for Advances in Religion and Science (CSAIRAS) and the Center of Theological Inquiry (CTI), among others.

9. Even more exciting is the possibility for a new theology called the theology of science. Professor Ralph Wendell Burhoe described this vision:

> It is still my bet that at several points in the next few years and decades the traditional theological and religious communities will find the scientific revelations a gold mine, and that by early in the third millennium A.D. a fantastic revitalization and universalization of religion will sweep the world. The ecumenical power will come from a universalized and credible theology and related religious practices, not from the politics of dying institutions seeking strength in pooling their weaknesses.
>
> I cannot imagine a more important bonanza for theologians and the future of religion than the information lode revealed by the scientific community . . . It provides us with a clear connection between human values, including our highest religious values, and the cosmic scheme of things.
>
> My prophecy, then, is that God talk, talk about the supreme determiner of human destiny, will in the next century increasingly be fostered by the scientific community.[20]

10. Another new phenomenon is the number of books on theology being written by mathematicians, physicists, biologists, and other natural scientists. Some scientists are reporting the results of their research on the human results of profound religious experience, some of which suggests observable effects of divine creativity in the world. For example, Sir Alister Hardy, the zoologist at Manchester College, Oxford, published a six-volume series on the nature of religious experience. Journals such as *Zygon* were founded to publish articles on the relationship between science and religion and have become well estab-

lished and well recognized for a high standard of excellence in scholarship. One of the most encouraging hopes for the future is to see a fulfillment of William James's wish: "Let empiricism once become associated with religion . . . and I believe that a new era of religion as well as of science will be ready to begin." Perhaps it already has.

11. An age of experimental theology may be beginning. This term is used to indicate efforts to gain understanding of the power of spiritual practices by concentrating on observable data resulting from spiritual experiences. Will following this approach open up religious concepts to rigorous empirical scrutiny? This should be an appealing notion even for skeptics. For example, the astronomer Carl Sagan wrote:

> It was an astonishing insight by Albert Einstein, central to the theory of general relativity, that gravitation could be understood by setting the contracted Riemann-Christoffel tensor equal to zero. But this contention was accepted only because one could work out the detailed mathematical consequences of the equations, see where it made predictions different from those of Newtonian gravitation, and then turn to experiment to see which way Nature votes. In three remarkable experiments—the deflection of starlight when passing near the sun; the motion of the orbit of Mercury, the planet nearest to the sun; and the red shift of spectral lines in a strong stellar gravitation field—Nature voted for Einstein. But without these experimental tests, very few physicists would have accepted general relativity. There are many hypotheses in physics of almost comparable brilliance and elegance that have been rejected because they did not survive such a confrontation with experiment. In my view, the human condition would be greatly improved if such confrontations and willingness to reject hypotheses were a regular part of our social, political, economic, religious and cultural lives.[21]

12. It is generally acknowledged in scientific circles that what we refer to as the laws of nature are more appropriately described as pro-

visional attempts to describe or model the way that things really are. The concept of provisionality is helpful, because it is not uncommon that a scientist will collect new data or propose a new theory that will modify or marginalize the older perspective. In general, scientists are ready to test and accept new ideas that enhance the foundation of science and build on it.

13. It is clear that very careful sensitivity and care will be required if such an approach were to be used by religious communities that cherish deep insights based on their core traditions. Therefore, in general, the better approach may be to search for ways to enrich and supplement religious traditions, rather than to consider them as in any way superseded by new concepts.

14. Why should spiritual people be less willing than scientists to listen sympathetically to new discoveries? Is such resistance a reflection not of religion but of human egotism?

15. Does the possibility of additional spiritual information depend upon scientists humble enough to admit that the unseen is vastly greater than the seen and upon theologians humble enough to admit that some older concepts of god may need to grow? Both hopefully can develop a vastly larger cosmology and wider, deeper theology, especially by working in creative dialog.

16. No one can foresee exactly which research projects for spiritual progress should be undertaken, or even the specific form that the most fruitful empirical inquiry might take. Nor can anyone foresee which experiments will prove fruitful. Explorations can be far more fruitful over the long term than their initiators can foresee. For example, when research in electricity began in the 18th century, no one could have predicted it would lead to indoor lighting, telephones, x-rays, television, interplanetary exploration, computation and the Internet. Research experience in the physical sciences shows that the

great majority of projects result in no useful invention. Surely, many attempts at developing spiritually significant research programs will end up empty-handed. But should this be considered a fundamental problem or simply a useful challenge? Great insights often are very hard to gain, and rare. Dr. Paul Ehrlich experimented with 606 chemicals before finding Salvarsan, the first cure for syphilis, called the magic bullet. In natural science, research is largely a matter of trial and error. So, it is often only through multitudes of experiments that key insights which open up whole new fields can be formulated and tested.

17. Therefore, no one can predict in advance what discoveries will be made by possible fruitful research in areas which may yield important insights and contribute to spiritual progress. The important thing is to get started and start accumulating insights based on experience. Institutions willing to finance research can welcome project proposals and then select the few that seem likely to offer the best results. Where and how to undertake research may be learned from earlier research and from the free flow of information between researchers. Since everything is so new and there are so few models to imitate, should this process of ongoing self-inquiry become the normal method? For example, experiments in physical science that yield reproducible results, of course, may not provide an appropriate paradigm for experiments appropriate for research in spiritual experiences in human beings. Is it possible, however, that a statistical approach may yield limited results in a range of spiritual matters, just as sociological patterns are determined by studies of large groups of people or aggregates of similar events? This is a common approach in the field of epidemiology where the most important insights do not involve deterministic predictability. For example, statistical surveys have convinced most people that the risk of contracting lung cancer is increased ten times for long-term cigarette smokers as compared with nonsmokers.

18. At first, not all religious leaders may welcome an experimental approach which may seem to supplement tradition. The first important challenge may be to demonstrate the benefits of spiritual progress as a way to invigorate religious believers and the life and vigor of their communities.

19. God promises to reveal himself to those who seek. If the seekers are physicists, then physics progresses more in its own realm than the church does in its realm. Can theology, once called the queen of the sciences, also use appropriate empirical methods of research? Can theology learn anything from the statistical methods of science? If that is possible, maybe it can become an adventure in the invention of research projects leading to the discovery and proof of facts about life in the spiritual universe. Likewise, should researchers in spiritual matters try out many different forms of inquiry and not be easily discouraged either? Researchers in fields like biology have yet discovered only a fraction of what may be known. So, researchers about the Infinite might not expect to produce systematic understanding that is comprehensive and unchanging. Exercising humility appropriate to the subject of their inquiry, they may hope to discover only a little more about humankind's relation to its creator. Open-minded questioning and open-minded faith are quite similar. Both derive from humility. Both affirm that most is unknown and thereby keep the door open to further investigation and progress. Should worshipers of every faith seek and welcome opportunities to demonstrate open-mindedness and a hunger to learn within a framework of continual change, modification and improvement?

20. Over six centuries ago, John Duns Scotus taught that the human intellect can know god through natural reason only up to a point, for human knowledge about the Infinite cannot itself be infinite. Mere human intellect can discover a few more spiritual truths to sup-

plement miraculous illuminations; and even then human intellect will comprehend very little of the Infinite.

21. It is humble to consider science as a guide for religion, but perhaps such an approach may be fruitful beyond what an initial assessment might suggest. Scientific progress in the 20th century has been astonishingly productive in unveiling aspects of reality. Perhaps it can in some humble ways be a gold mine for revitalizing religion in the 21st century.

22. The scientific concepts that first appear inimical to religions at a primitive level of analysis may in the end contribute to the development of new universal symbols and languages that can help keep human values and religious concepts viable. Burhoe agrees with Anthony Wallace that religion

> is the very center of man's most advanced evolutionary thrust to find order or organization, governing his overall attitudes and behaviors with respect not only to himself and his fellow men but also with regard to the ultimate realities of that cosmos in which he lives and moves and has his being.

23. In general, should discussion about divinity in the 21st century take place in close contact with the scientific community if it is to be widely relevant to our future society? Is it wise to begin those discussions now? Theologians pursuing spiritual progress may benefit from close contact with research scientists and may benefit from serious engagement with the research frontiers of active scientific exploration.

24. Is it possible that the earth may enter a new era of spirit beyond the noosphere even more exciting than Burhoe's prediction regarding the theology of science? Can theology of science be one step toward that era of spirit? As we have said earlier, the development of humans on earth may not be the end of creativity but only the beginning of it. Always, it has been difficult to imagine what would come

next. However, the multitude of discoveries in the 20th century about things previously unseen points toward the likelihood of even more amazing discoveries, hopefully including spiritual discoveries.

25. Eighty years ago, Professor Charles P. Steinmetz, director of General Electric Laboratories in Schenectady, said that when the great discoveries of the 20th century go down in history, they will not be in natural science but in the realm of the spirit. Eighty years later we see little evidence of these discoveries. Could the reason be that we have poured vastly more money and manpower into the natural sciences? Are we still blind to the possibility that the ever new discoveries in natural sciences are actually data revealing the nature of the universal creative Spirit?

26. Can we try to devise some possible research projects in religion that might resemble current research in the physical world of science, medicine, economics and politics? To serve as illustrations, here are a few various possibilities:

A. EXPLORING LINKS BETWEEN RELIGIOSITY AND LENGTH AND QUALITY OF LIFE

Various research results have shown quite an extraordinary association between religious involvement, broadly considered, and likelihood of death among elderly people. At present, the reason for this association is unclear. However, it is quite substantial, almost a 50% reduction in the risk of dying during follow-up and close to a 30% reduction when corrected for other known predictors of mortality. This effect on survival is equivalent in magnitude to that of not smoking versus smoking cigarettes (about seven years of added life). Does such a linkage between even average involvement in religion and health show a need for careful analysis to illuminate what is not yet known?

B. RESEARCHING THE BENEFITS OF FORGIVENESS

Do you think that forgiveness and reconciliation give tremendous potential for spiritual progress? So much unhappiness and persistent violence in the world are due to unresolved conflict. Vast resources are lost to individuals and to businesses and governments due to lack of an ability to prevent conflicts and to put an end to their festering persistence. The spiritual practice of forgiveness has the potential to heal wounds and stop conflicts, but it is not so widely appreciated and practiced. The John Templeton Foundation helped to start in 1997 a major program of sponsorship for research on the spiritual principle of forgiveness and its application for reconciliation to prevent, mediate or resolve conflicts. This program involves developing a coalition of donors to provide a total of ten million dollars to initiate pioneering research efforts across a wide range of subjects, including basic research in primatology, genetics, neuroscience, studies in marriage and family therapy, medical recovery, treatment of addictions, reconciliation in the criminal justice system and studies of a wide variety of forgiveness intervention experiments.

C. EXTRAORDINARY SPIRITUAL HEALING

Several church denominations have collected thousands of well-documented cases of what is described as divine healing. Typically, these attestations involve observations of radical spontaneous remission of serious life-threatening disease. Were it possible to clinically confirm and scientifically understand such phenomena, it could offer a significant potential advance for medical science. The key issue in such studies would be humility, both with respect to the challenge of biased advocacy by uncritical believers on the one hand, and closed-minded radical skepticism on the other hand. This topic offers another possibility for spiritual progress.

D. Possible Benefits of Spiritual Hope and Positive-Mindedness in Healing

Some doctors observe large differentials in patients' rate of healing following similar operations by as much as a factor of three. Can a positive mind promote the faster modes of healing for reasons that are not entirely clear? Some cases of religious people who have great hope and optimism in the face of medical adversity, indicate that spiritual attitude can be an important positive factor in healing. Can this be studied to better understand the phenomenon and help people generally to heal faster and be more resistant to disease? For overviews generally of medically important insights linking health and healing with religion and spirituality, see the following books: Herbert Benson, *Timeless Healing: The Power of Biology and Belief* (1997); Harold G. Koenig, *The Healing Power of Faith: Science Explores Medicine's Last Great Frontier* (1999); Harold G. Koenig, *Is Religion Good for Your Health?* (1997); D. B. Larson et al., *Scientific Research on Spirituality and Health: A Consensus Report* (1998); D. B. Larson and S. S. Larson, *The Forgotten Factor in Physical and Mental Health: What Does the Research Show?* (1994); D. B. Larson, *The Faith Factor, Volume 2: An Annotated Bibliography of Systematic Reviews and Clinical Research on Spiritual Subjects* (1993); D. A. Matthews and D. B. Larson, *The Faith Factor: An Annotated Bibliography of Clinical Research on Spiritual Subjects Vols. 1-4* (1993-1996); Harold G. Koenig, M. McCullough and D. B. Larson *Handbook of Religion and Health: A Century of Research Reviewed* (2000).

E. RESEARCH ON SPIRITUALLY ENCOURAGED CHARACTER QUALITIES SUCH AS HUMILITY, SENSE OF PURPOSE, FUTURE MINDEDNESS, LOVE AND THANKFULNESS.

Can participation in the religious life sometimes be a strong motivator and inspiration in the formation of broadly beneficial qualities of good character? Can this process be studied and understood so that people will better comprehend the benefits of religious research and participation within the life of a religious community? What experiments are possible and statistics collectable about such spiritual traits?

F. RESEARCHING SPIRITUAL FACTORS WHICH HELP PEOPLE TO FIND JOY IN LIFE

St. Paul says that joy is one of the fruits of the spirit. We all know from experience that a joyful spirit is a wonderful asset to anybody and that it can help greatly to surmount adversity as well as to create beneficial opportunities for others. Many spiritual autobiographies describe the process of religious conversion or enlightenment as a kind of discovery of joy. Among the most famous of these is the description recorded by the Oxford literary scholar and writer C. S. Lewis, whose autobiography is entitled *Surprised by Joy*. Can research into the phenomenon of spiritual joyfulness lead to helpful insights both for religious people and nonreligious people? Helping people to be joyful is yet another idea of possible spiritual research. Which people radiate happiness? Could scholars or researchers devise interesting and beneficial research on these questions?

G. SPIRITUAL TRANSFORMATION

Christians often refer to a favorite verse in the third chapter of the Gospel of John, describing one or more transformative events in their lives as an experience of having been born again. Christians also describe a variety of important experiences as being filled with the spirit. Their descriptions often concur in asserting that their lives are no longer the same and have been transformed for the better. Independent observers often attest to these changes as well. Can study of the nature of such changes offer another possibility for developing spiritual progress based on improved understanding of, and appreciation for, spiritually transformative experiences?

H. PSYCHIATRIC HEALTH

Do persons who become charismatic Christians through the experience of Pentecost need psychiatric help less than they did before? Is there something about professing one's religion or confessing one's sins, that is, discussing one's interior life openly with others, that reduces the need for a psychiatrist's couch? Perhaps scientists could collect statistics on the frequency of visits to psychiatrists before and after the charismatic experience.

I. HELPING SAVE "AT-RISK" YOUTH FROM DELINQUENCY

Can beneficial aspects of religious involvement help to save at-risk youth from becoming entangled in lives of crime with high rates of violent death, imprisonment, drug addiction, depression, lack of employment and lifelong inability to cope? A recent systematic review conducted by the Center for Civic Innovation at the Manhattan Institute in New York offers interesting insights. The review surveyed the relevance and summarized broadly common findings of forty articles that had considered religion as a study variable. These studies had been culled from 402 major studies of delinquency published in top ranked journals between the years 1980 and 1997. (Thus only about 10% of studies had considered religiosity at all.) Seventy-five percent of the studies that did consider religiosity showed significantly decreased delinquency in association with religiousness in one form or another. Do these findings suggest that various involvement in religious community life may substantially reduce risk for children who grow up in dangerous high-risk environments? Can developments of high-quality research in this field exemplify another dimension of spiritual progress?

J. AN INSTINCT TO WORSHIP

Apparently, there has never been a tribe who did not worship. Why have about fifty thousand new worship sects arisen in the 20th century? Has such instinct been researched scientifically? Does this give evidence of some mysterious realities which could be researched? What are the causes, nature of benefits, from this urge? What causes a sect to grow into a religion?

Every tribe was awestruck by storm lightning bolts for over four hundred centuries, but only since 1800 has science research discovered amazing new benefits from electronics. If equal research expense were to be focused on evidences of basic spiritual realities, could the benefits be even more amazing?

27. These are only a few examples of the types of research projects in science and religion that institutes, academies and seminaries could undertake.

28. Research developed using rigorous and careful scientific methodology can be convincing to well-educated leaders. Such an approach avoids the problem of advocacy. It presents religion, its benefits as well as its flaws, before careful, honest and objective scrutiny. It encourages what is beneficial and opens up what is not to the opportunity for im-

provements. Can this research bring great ongoing vitality to the world's religions over the long term? Should people who love god diligently work to devise thousands of appropriate, theologically and scientifically acceptable experiments? Also, should they write articles for science journals and collect bibliographies of experimental research of this kind in the study of spiritual laws and observable effects of the unseen spirit?

29. Why should we think human happiness is the ultimate purpose? Who can be so self-centered as to imagine that personal happiness or health or long life for one new species on one little planet can be the final purpose of divine creativity? Can it belittle divine purpose to think our species can soon reach final answers? Or instead, is each new discovery always a door to more searching? Who can be so self-centered as to think that our particular species can ever reach final answers? Does evidence say that mysteries are always multiplying faster than solutions? Is it more thrilling and more fruitful to worship awesome and increasing mysteries than old discoveries? For unending and accelerating search, what better words can be found than "open-mindedness" or "the humble approach"?

30. A scientific approach has the benefit of being reality-focused and disciplined in relation to change. As a bishop of Oxford once remarked, "the church that is married to the spirit of the age will be widow to the next generation." So the development of new concepts in theology developed in close connection with rigorous science differs from unconstrained free thinking. The difference involves differentiating between ideological enthusiasm versus following a careful, sober and skeptically minded process of analysis, critical testing and verification. Such a careful, humble approach helps ensure that experiments related to spiritual matters are done in a manner that can win respect among the best-educated people.

31. Perhaps in due course respected religious journals will take pride in publishing surveys overviewing progress in religion as a result of such studies and also covering how far discoveries of astronomers and physicists may contribute to theological insight. If the voice of science, however indirectly, is one of the voices of god, should it be listened to with reverence? If laws of the spirit are fragments of knowledge about divinity, so also in their way are the laws of nature. Can churches and other religious groups honor scientists committed to studying the divine as it manifests itself in the physical world? Can seminaries play an important leadership role inviting leading scientists to lecture and to offer courses on progress in their fields of particular potential relevance for theology and religious training?

32. Possibly through careful and humble research we may be able to realize aspects of a hope expressed by Henry Drummond in the 1850s, namely, that the artificial sense of a split between the natural and the supernatural can be transcended by improved insight. He suggested that

> what is required to draw Science and Religion together again—for they began the centuries hand in hand—is the disclosure of the naturalness of the supernatural. Then, and not till then, will men see how true it is, that to be loyal to all of Nature, they must be loyal to the part defined as spiritual. . . . And even as the contribution of Science to Religion is the vindication of the naturalness of the Supernatural, so the gift of Religion to Science is the demonstration of the supernaturalness of the Natural. Thus, as the Supernatural becomes slowly Natural, will also the Natural become slowly Supernatural, until in the impersonal authority of Law men everywhere recognize the Authority of God.[22]

33. Drummond's dream is a noble and visionary one; will it be worthwhile seeing how far it can go? If divinity is real and includes all things, then should we not assume that the cosmos does possess a rich-

ness and strangeness which may surprise us in very subtle and interesting ways? By pursuing such possibilities rigorously and carefully and in a spirit of mutually respectful adventure, it might be discovered that members of both the scientific and religious communities can find productive common ground upon which to help each other.

34. Finding such common ground may not be so difficult in the 21st century as it may have seemed a century earlier. Henry Margenau, professor of physics at Yale, wrote that

> science now acknowledges as real a host of entities that cannot be described completely in mechanistic or materialistic terms. For these reasons the demands which science makes upon religion when it examines religion's claims to truth have become distinctly more modest; the conflict between science and religion has become less sharp, and the strain of science upon religion has been greatly relieved. In fact, a situation seems to prevail in which the theologian can seriously listen to a scientist expounding his methodology with some expectation that the latter may ring a sympathetic chord. It is not altogether out of the question that the rules of scientific methodology are now sufficiently wide and flexible to embrace some forms of religion within the scientific domain.[23]

35. Can mutual dialogue between science and religion, combined with very high-quality studies demonstrating the fruitfulness of such a rapprochement, put to rest the old and unhelpful notion that science and religion are irreconcilably at war with one another? That can be real progress, both scientific and spiritual!

CHAPTER NINE

Love, Humility and Free Competition Accelerate Discoveries

1. The humble approach does not promise either security or ease; it is risky and strenuous pioneering research. Pioneering is not likely to be welcome by the weak of heart or will. Developers of the humble approach may be persons who are strong-hearted and clear-minded, those adventurers who are unafraid of competition and struggle. The humble approach asks of its followers a firm dedication to freedom and a vigilant suspicion of security. As Benjamin Franklin put it in America's revolutionary days, "Anyone who gives up a little freedom for a little security does not deserve either."

2. One of the greatest developments in human history has been the increasing possibility for each person to have the freedom to learn, to grow and to design his or her own life. This is a relatively new phenomenon. Throughout recorded history, most governments have been authoritarian, characterized by the rule of a few over the many. Such governments have allowed little popular influence on decision-making in domestic laws or foreign policy and little freedom of religion or speech. Most societies have not been open to new concepts.

3. Beginning around the time of the Renaissance, more emphasis was given to the expression of individual personality, to the notion that opportunity is a vital human concern and to the idea that personal re-

searching is more important than collective conformity dictated from on high. Such notions eventually helped lead to the Reformation—a great breakthrough in religious freedom and competition. The freedom revolutions of the 18th century, leading to new scientific discoveries, produced the free world as we know it today, a world in which the individual is important, where a man's or woman's opinion will be respectfully considered, where each person has the right to choose the basics of a productive life, career, marriage partner, school, religion, place of residence and free expression.

4. Freedom fosters the kind of constructive competition that makes progress possible. When the creativity, ingenuity and competitive efforts of individuals are set free, the result can be progress and prosperity beyond anything ever before imagined. In the free world amazing progress is beginning in the areas of education, religion, production, science, art and literature. Inventions are being multiplied and culture is being enriched. God's ongoing creation seems to favor free, tolerant, open-minded individuals as helpers toward progress. This individual freedom is enhanced by other freedoms—those of worship, free speech, free enterprise and the right to own property. It is interesting that god does not force his good upon us. Instead, god gives us the free will to claim or reject the blessings of life.

5. Only god knows whether the bounteous acceleration of our progress and increase in knowledge over the past four hundred years will continue. It certainly could, unless it is halted by the greatest roadblock to human progress and happiness: authoritarian institutional power, as in excessive government. Freedom does, of course, require a measure of government. As Jefferson put it, government is instituted to "secure" our liberties. But excessive government, warned the author of the Declaration of Independence, is the chief destroyer of freedom. Government maintains freedom only to the extent that it gives each

person freedom from monopolies and from domination by others and protection from criminals. But too much government intervention in the economic, cultural or spiritual life of its citizens inhibits that freedom and progress. Perhaps more research needs to be done to identify which government activities protect freedom and which ones restrict it. Lincoln believed that government should do for its people only those things that they could not do for themselves.

6. Ironically, it may well be the case that most people in the world are uneasy with the idea of individual freedom. In Erich Fromm's phrase, many seek an "escape from freedom." Such people may feel comfortable or secure only under strong authority. This could occur when a dictator or even an authoritarian church tells people exactly what to do and think. Perhaps this desire for being led is one reason why democracy has not yet proven to be a popular form of government in every nation and every church. Awareness of this common desire may also be the reason that many of America's founders thought a democratic experiment would be short-lived.

7. Maybe communism established a place in people's minds and hearts as a consequence of the vacuum created by failure of religions to develop and progress with the knowledge explosion. Maybe the communist threat served the purpose of contesting the increasing religious and social rigidities that occur when there are no great challenges to face. Adversity often seems to serve a creative purpose.

8. But communism is now becoming obsolete, because after the first revolutions, its doctrines became rigid and forbade change. In the rise of any new ideology, rigid doctrine leads only to the triumph of rigidity itself. This rigidity, however, leads to decay and obsolescence. Decay became evident in many communist countries because their governments prevented freedom in so many areas of personal life: economic, religious, intellectual and artistic. Being so earth-centered,

communism became as narrow-minded as the cosmologies of the ancients who pictured the universe extending for only a few thousand miles and enclosed within the star-studded spheres of the heavens.

9. Communism was founded on hatred between the classes and envy of those to whom god gives more talents. That being the case, it was unlikely to uplift human nature. Communism substituted the collective structure of government for the individual as the giver of welfare to those in need. But the greater blessing from giving goes not to the receiver but to the loving giver. Jesus said, "It is more blessed to give than to receive" (Acts 20:35 KJV). The giver is the one who is more uplifted and spiritualized by the gift. When giving is channeled through government by force, it has an opposite effect on the producer whose produce is forcibly given. Forced charity does not uplift either the giver or the receiver. It dehumanizes and hinders the spiritual growth of all the people. Forced charity may be better than no charity, but it is a pitiful substitute.

10. Some leaders once hoped that the World Council of Churches would lead to a world union of institutional churches. Many other writers, especially some of the Hindu faith, advocated a union of all religions. Should we not make every effort to tolerate each other, listen to each other and eventually love each other? Of course, many benefits flow also from sharing literature and information with each other and from the development of facilities to help us lovingly listen to each other.

11. But could centralized authority from a bureaucracy of united world churches be the prelude to stagnation? Would growth of religion best be stimulated not by union but through freedom and competition? Originality and discovery derive from variety, not from uniformity. If each denomination of every faith sent missionaries to every other community lovingly to explain and share its vision with others,

then would we all learn more? If our concepts truly convey the divine, then they will not suffer in competition with other concepts. What a happy competition it would be if each of us were lovingly trying to give to the other our holy treasures. How selfish it would be for us not to witness to others or not to send missionaries abroad! But likewise, if other religions or denominations want lovingly to witness to us, should we not receive their unselfish missionaries with our minds open and with gratitude and shared joy?

12. Among professional scientists there is usually a friendly rivalry between those holding to different theories or belonging to different schools of thought. Should not churches foster the same sort of constructive competition? If they do not, they may appear old-fashioned and soon become irrelevant. God's long creative process has always led to greater diversity. Let us rejoice in diversity and avoid establishing any monolithic religion. By spirited and loving competition, will not the basic spiritual principles be both purified and strengthened?

13. Progress comes from constructive competition, and churches and religions can benefit greatly from it. By free competition the wheat is gradually separated from the chaff. A beneficial religion should welcome competition because when it is put to the test, the beneficial will survive and grow. Only an inferior religion needs to discourage competition, lest its inferiority be exposed for all the world to see. The long history of evolution of plant and animal varieties would seem to indicate that competition is one of god's chosen methods of developing novel and fruitful forms of life in his accelerating creativity. Why should it be different in the realm of spirit and religion?

14. Tolerance may be a divine virtue, but it could also become a vehicle for apathy. Millions of people are thoroughly tolerant toward diverse religions, but rarely do such people go down in history as creators, benefactors or leaders of progress. A far more constructive use of tolerance

would be to promote humility so that we might be more inclined to listen with an open heart and an inquiring mind. Should we not desire to have our neighbor share insights and try to convey to us the brilliant light that has transformed his life—the fire in his soul? Why settle for a least-common-denominator type of religion based on tolerance alone? More than tolerance, we need constructive competition. When persons on fire for a great gospel compete lovingly to give their finest treasures to each other, will not everyone benefit? If we enthusiastically share the inspiring highlights of each faith and church, then are we not all richer? On our daily upward struggle toward love for one another and union with our creator, do we need all the inspiration and insight that every child of god can give us?

15. In summarizing the views of Teilhard de Chardin, N. Max Wildiers suggests that there are two ways of unifying mankind—by coercion or by sympathy and affection. The truly creative force is a combination of sympathy and affection. Even at lower levels than the human, these forces operate to unify and create the universe. They are, says Wildiers,

> the constructive forces in the cosmos as a whole. The atoms were impelled towards one another by an intrinsic affinity: and so the molecules came into being. The cells coalesced; and thence the great diversity of organisms appeared.[24]

16. Another area in life where the benefit of competition is being undermined is in the lack of teaching of religion in schools. In recent years American schools have come to teach mainly secular rather than religious concepts. Is it any wonder that misbehavior is increasing? The Templeton Foundations give honors to the schools and colleges which still consider it their first duty to teach honesty, ethics, character, morals, self-control, noble purpose and religion. Most churches seem content to devote only one hour a week in Sunday school to teach our children principles governing spiritual growth. Many Sunday schools

rely only on amateur teachers and require no homework, no prizes, no grades or tests. How woefully ignorant our children would be if we relied on such methods to teach history or science! Little wonder that we are said to be rearing a generation of moral and spiritual weaklings.

17. Until the 20th century, most colleges and universities were founded and supported by religious groups. Often the main purpose was to prepare priests or ministers for their lifework. Most schools for children were founded and taught by religious people. Now, most of these schools and colleges, in the name of impartiality, have abandoned responsibility for teaching religion in favor of secular subjects. The list of colleges and universities is filled with the names of formerly famous religious schools.

18. In the name of equality or social justice, governments increasingly dominate educational policies and diminish the viability of church-supported schools. In the United States, the courts today rule that the Constitution forbids religion in public schools, even though the authors of the Constitution had no such intent. The men who framed the Constitution of the United States would be dumbfounded by the Supreme Court decision that forbade worship in public schools. The founders of our nation intended to ensure free and fair competition among religions, not to stamp out religion altogether. Their efforts to separate church and state were not efforts to abolish religious education in the classroom. The current practice of near total omission of religion from schools prevents free competition. The net effect may be to imply that only secular knowledge is respectable. Are new generations being educated to be intellectual and cultural adults but spiritual and ethical infants?

19. Are there are ways, however, to keep religion in our schools without favoring one religion or one denomination over the others? Methods have been devised to allow each child, or its parents, to

choose from a broad spectrum of religious studies—from traditional world religions to atheism. Would it not be possible, for example, for each school to provide a room which could be used at chosen hours for thirty minutes weekly or more often by various religious or nonreligious groups wanting to present their beliefs or to engage in worship? Students or their parents could then choose which to attend for such thirty minutes of spiritual education weekly or more often.

20. Is it not possible that constructive competition is god's law for development in the universe because it functions to weed out the useless and to stimulate change for the better? Does god's pattern of evolutionary development provide both the occasion and the mechanism for progress? If we do not have free competition among ideas, even religious ideas, the old and established theories may never be improved. Old ideas and routines may never have to defend themselves. Some may survive long after their time of usefulness. Do you learn more when you speak or when you listen? Does an open mind or a closed mind learn more? Are multiplying mysteries more worshipful than old certainties?

21. This is what the humble approach thrives on: an open mind, a willingness to admit there might be alternative articulations of truth just as valuable as ours and the enthusiasm to compete constructively with others—to search, to discover and to create the better and better societies and religions of the future.

22. Should we remind ourselves once more that to embark upon the humble approach is to ask for constructive competition and the testing of ideas? To assure that the competition is fair, maybe no church, no school, no government should seek to impose (rather just offer) its system upon others who do not share the same concepts. Do church members, students and citizens need a healthy and open-minded freedom so that, unfettered by the tyranny of forced conformity, they can examine

the rich and increasing variety of ideas in god's universe? Should we be constantly vigilant against any person, group, institution or political party that would tyrannize our lives? To encourage humility, research and free competition, Thomas Jefferson proposed "eternal enmity over every form of tyranny over the mind of man."

23. Happiness sought eludes. Happiness given returns. Why does the conscious pursuit of our own happiness fail? Maybe because real happiness is mainly a by-product of trying to give happiness to others. Ralph Waldo Trine has said:

> A corollary of the great principle already enunciated might be formulated thus: there is no such thing as finding true happiness by searching for it directly. It must come, if it comes at all, indirectly, or by the service, the love and the happiness we give to others. So there is no such thing as finding true greatness by searching for it directly. It always, without a single exception, has come indirectly in this same way, and it is not at all probable that this great eternal law is going to be changed to suit any particular case or cases. Then recognize it, put your life into harmony with it, and reap the rewards of its observance, or fail to recognize it and pay the penalty accordingly: for the law itself will remain unchanged. Life is not, we may say, for mere passing pleasure, but for the highest unfoldment that one can attain to, the noblest character that one can grow and for the greatest service that one can render to all mankind. In this, however, we will find the highest pleasure, for in this the only real pleasure lies.[25]

24. If we use the humble approach, should we radiate love and happiness as faithfully as the sun radiates light and warmth? As sunlight is a creative life-giving source, so can our love be a creative source of increased vitality and bright ideas. God is said to be the source of love. Love cannot flow in unless it also flows out. Does the spirit of god resemble a stream of water and are god's followers like

many beautiful fountains fed by this river of water? Can each one of us be such a fountain if we keep the channel open, so that god's spirit can flow through us helping others receive and learn to give unselfish love? What science research can help everyone understand the basic invisible reality called unselfish love unlimited?

25. Without god as our source of inspiration, we are not likely to bring forth much good. We may never learn to radiate love as long as we love ourselves selfishly, for if we are characterized by self-concern, we radiate self-concern.

> Jesus then said to his disciples, "If anyone wishes to be a follower of mine, he must leave self behind; he must take up his cross and come with me. Whoever cares for his own safety is lost; but if a man will let himself be lost for my sake, he will find his true self." (Matthew 16:24–25 NEB)

26. God loves us all equally and unceasingly. Is this a basic eternal reality? Should we seek always to let god's love shine forth like the light inside an electric bulb illuminating all our habitation? Emil Brunner wrote:

> Every human relationship which does not express love is abnormal. In Jesus Christ we are told that this love is the whole meaning of our life, and is also its foundation. Here the Creator reveals himself as the One who has created us in love, by love, for love. He reveals to us our true nature, and He gives it back to us.[26]

27. Rufus Matthew Jones taught that those who worship god are empowered by the Spirit and that religion is not a burden but rather a means of being lifted up to new heights of joy and philanthropic achievement. The divine spirit moves into your life and makes it over from within so that all things are seen in a new light, and love for all becomes the spontaneous expression of a spirit-filled soul. If we de-

pend too much on the visible world, or trust our own ability too much or love ourselves excessively, we may never learn to radiate love. Instead we may radiate self-concern, egotism and arrogance. Ironically, egotism may not allow us to find our true selves. Can self-concern cause us to miss our true self of grace and generosity and thus tend to sever our links with eternal love? The self we admire so greatly becomes a diminished version of the total self that might have been.

28. The ultimate conceit is to assume that no mind can be greater than human mind. How could humans be so egotistical as to believe that no other being in the vast universe can be purposeful and consciously creative? Or how can we assume that creatures on other planets may not have learned more about divinity than we? Surely humanity's multitudinous creations are tiny and few compared with what the mind that created us may have fashioned in other galaxies and in unseen realms and in dimensions beyond today's limited human concepts.

29. The humble search for god continues in many new ways, seeking to recreate and revitalize all religions. Have we ever met a person who was helped to grow spiritually by turning away from all religion? Do those who turn away become better persons, more useful or more high-minded? Would it not be more beneficial for humankind if persons to whom god has given keen intellects use their talents for researching concepts to enlarge our understanding and love of god?

30. The humble approach includes a vision of spiritual progress as limitless, unending research that calls us to do our best work, to serve others, to love, to aspire beyond the merely human. According to the humble approach, love leads to charity. Charity is not the same as forms of welfare dependence. Giving welfare to the unemployed, although good for the soul of the giver, is not good for the soul of the receiver. The greater charity is to help a person join the ranks of the givers rather than be trapped forever in the position of receiver. When the desire to

give replaces the desire to get, a person may exchange an attitude of childishness for one of maturity. Just as when one nation gives food to another nation longer than for relief of temporary tragedies, the donations do no spiritual good for the recipient nation. In fact, human nature is such that the receivers often become envious, demanding and resentful. Such attitudes can shrink the souls of people. Evidence indicates that "safety nets" are more compassionate and beneficial if provided by private charities competing for government subsidies by showing cost-effectiveness and teaching self-help methods.

31. The greater charity is to help the people of a poor nation to learn the traits which lead to prosperity, such as trustworthiness, hard work, honesty, free competition, thrift and the Golden Rule. Any poor nation can be converted to amazing prosperity rather quickly and lastingly if its people and government adopt wholeheartedly these six virtues. Not only is this a way to material prosperity, but also to spiritual wealth. The more loving gift to the poor is not money but opportunity.

32. The wealth of a nation comes not from natural resources but from what is in the minds and hearts of its people. People pursuing the humble approach express their love in charity to prevent or to alleviate suffering and to elevate the recipients of their love. Feeding the hungry, caring for the sick, clothing the naked are all compassionate in the short term; but in the long term, the real charity is to help the poor learn the spiritual traits that lead to progress, productivity, prosperity, dignity and happiness. Bestowing technology and know-how on people in poor nations is a blessing; but the lasting blessing may be people who can radiate love and joy as they research and teach the basic spiritual realities, which then lead to progress, improved skills, spiritual wealth and also material prosperity. Who can devise additional scientific or statistical research to test these concepts?

CHAPTER TEN

Can Earth Serve
as a School?

1. Almost all of the enduring religions speak about life after death. Some Buddhists and some Hindus expect no heaven or hell as the Christians, Muslims and Jews do but instead expect continual rebirth until achieving a blissful nirvana.

2. Most nonreligious people speak of each human as not only body and mind but also an individual self, a soul, a personality, no two of which are exactly alike. Whatever you choose to name it, both religious and nonreligious people want that self to be educated and continually improved. Often, this is called character education. Even people not interested in spiritual research can often be enthusiastic for character education being used as an ounce of prevention for miseries, which can be more cost effective than a pound of cure. By research could more and more productive ways be found for improvement of self, soul or personality?

3. When scientific methods are applied to the question of evidences for why humans were created, such research can explore needs for and methods and benefits of education of character or self or spirit. Can research applied to progress of individual character explore the evidences that our lives on earth may serve the purpose of character education? Even that earth can in some ways serve as a school?

4. Is character education an example of the old wisdom that "an ounce of prevention is worth a pound of cure?" Is it less expensive and more beneficial for everyone to learn character improvement in schools than to rehabilitate those two million Americans in jail in 1999?

5. This chapter opens up for research the usefulness of earthly life as a method of schooling and research on possibilities for improving such schooling.

> Ernest O. Martin in 1962 reflected on the significance of spiritual development, the formation of a heavenly character. This is the purpose of life on this planet, which Swedenborg spoke of as a seminary for heaven. It is here that we grow into angelhood and begin to develop the potentialities that god sees within us. Heaven is essentially a quality of life, an inward condition or state in which men live in harmony with the will of god. And yet it is also a place—a real, tangible, substantial existence. Swedenborg's answer is that life is one. The natural world and the spiritual world are not two distinct, separate existences that have no relationship. We are spirits and from the day of our conception we are citizens of the spiritual world. Love, understanding, loyalty, friendship, patience, mercy—these are spiritual realities the Lord seeks to instill in our lives here and now. The natural world is the theater in which our spirits operate and develop and grow. It is here that our loves, our attitudes and our desires are molded and find expression. That is why god has placed us here.

6. A lifetime on earth may seem a slow way to educate a soul. And fifteen billion years may seem to us a slow way to erect the school building. However, to put things into perspective, let us remember that divinity may have created time also. Nels F. S. Ferré (1908–1972) often reminded us that god is not bound by time if he created not only our universe but also both space and time. What is the purpose of time? Is its role to make room for learning, for growth and for developing our ability to give love?

7. The Christian religion speaks often about the way in which the human experience on earth is to function as preparation. To progress spiritually can be to increase our love of god, or understanding of god, and love for his children. Although our body has a physical reality, can it be only a temporary dwelling place? Our physical body will some day die. But maybe death destroys only that fit for destruction. The butterfly developing in the chrysalis in due time splits open and abandons the dead chrysalis and flies away on wings of amazing beauty undreamed of by the chrysalis or the caterpillar.

8. Various major religions have described earth as a school. The Hindu *Bhagavad-Gita* ("Song of god") teaches:

> Whatever a man remembers at the last, when he is leaving the body, will be realized by him in the hereafter, because that will be what his mind has most constantly dwelt on during his life. Therefore you must remember me at all times and do your duty. If your mind and heart are set upon me constantly, you will come to me. Never doubt this. . . . I am the Atman that dwells in the heart of every mortal creature; I am the beginning, the lifespan, and the end of all. . . . one atom of myself sustains the universe.

9. Buddhism, teaching that the life of the spirit transcends the life of a man on earth, emphasizes that this life of the spirit is the only true reality and that on earth, people should strive to grow spiritually through exercising free-will, reason, love and meditation.

10. The Reverend Charles Neal in 1976 expressed his concept of life in a way that was informed both by his Christian heritage and by the science of his day:

> Who then are we? We are God's perfect children in the making. Each of us is evolving to perfection. But at this stage we do not yet have it made. Let us recognize that the universe is a cosmos. It is not slaphappy, disorganized, haphazard or accidental. It is an or-

derly system and its nature is to evolve. That is, to bring into the open through endless and infinitely slow degrees that which is already involved in it, namely perfect creation.[27]

11. In the 20th century Teilhard de Chardin, speaking from long years as a scientist, priest and poet, said, "It is a law of the universe that in all things there is prior existence. Before every form there is a prior, but lesser evolved form. Each one of us is evolving towards the godhead." Could it be that this evolving toward god is the fundamental purpose of our life on earth?

12. Now, if earth is a school for eternity, who are the teachers? Life is full of very considerable challenges and difficulties which present opportunities for learning and progress. Therefore, one teacher may be *adversity*. Could it be that adversity can play a constructive role in life? Could it be that without these experiences our education would be incomplete? Maybe from divine perspective, can the sorrows and tribulations of humans help to educate us for eternity?

13. How could a person understand divine joy or be thankful for heaven without previously experiencing the full range of earthly life? How could a person comprehend the joy of surrender to divine will if he or she never witnessed the hell men make on earth by trying to rely exclusively on self-will or the whims of another frail human being or of a soulless, power-based bureaucratic organization?

14. Given that life includes a measure of adversity, do most of us have a sense of how much growth can come through trial and self-discipline? On the other side of the ledger, is there a wealth of evidence indicating that too much prosperity without work weakens character and causes us to become self-centered? Does spiritual growth and happiness come from getting or from learning to give? Do people who give most readily grow most rapidly? Can scientist find statistics to test these possibilities?

15. As a good father does not do his son's homework for him, so our heavenly father does not excuse us from what helps us to grow. A good parent gives a child what is needed, not always what is desired. Should we not be thankful that god does not always give us the selfish or trivial things we ask for? St. Paul wrote:

> More than this: let us even exult in our present sufferings, because we know that suffering trains us to endure, and endurance brings proof that we have stood the test, and this proof is the ground of hope. Such a hope is no mockery, because God's love has flooded our inmost heart through the Holy Spirit he has given us. (Romans 5:3–5 NEB)

16. How do spiritual maturity and strength grow? Can spiritual growth take place through many means—through the application of human reason and research, through openness to divine revelation and through the diligent use of the various talents given to each of us? As the human body is developed through physical exercise, can our capacity for choosing good over evil be developed by spiritual exercise? In exercising our free will and choosing good, can we demonstrate that we are created in the image of god? By being a positive creator in the world in which we live, rather than a destroyer, can we help in the acceleration of divine creativity?

17. Can researchers discover what personalities are achieving heaven while on earth? Who can devise tests to discover which are the happier people and why? The major religions for many centuries have written hundreds of principles for character improvement, but can scientists begin rigorous research, especially by collecting statistics, to provide evidence for the usefulness of many spiritual principles? By character education, could most miseries be avoided?

18. Just as government is essentially a means of control over others, is one's religion essentially control over self? Can those who have

learned to put aside completely their selfish egos and become as little children enter into the kingdom of heaven? Is our job to be pure like a clean windowpane so that the truth and light of divinity can shine through, or like a static-free radio receiver through which divine music enters the world, when we are consciously aware of and thankful for multitudes of blessings? St. Paul wrote, "For we are God's handiwork, created in Christ Jesus to devote ourselves to the good deeds, for which God has designed us" (Ephesians 8:10 NEB).

19. Can spiritual growth be achieved in part by researches, that is, by overcoming our ignorance and self-centeredness until we are in tune with the divine? We must always be eager for further discoveries and new insights into both spiritual and natural phenomena. We should never imagine we know enough. Trine put it this way:

> Great spiritual truths—truths of the real life are the same in all ages, and will come to any man and any woman who will make the conditions whereby they can come. God speaks wherever he finds a humble listening ear, whether it be Jew or Gentile, Hindu or Parsee, American or East Indian, Christian or Bushman. It is the realm of the inner life that we should wisely give more attention to. The springs of life are all from within. We must make the right mental condition, and we must couple with it faith and expectancy. We should also give sufficient time in the quiet, that we may clearly hear and rightly interpret.[28]

20. Should not each of us work for self-improvement by prayer, worship, study and meditation? One of the spiritual principles seems to be that self-improvement comes mainly from trying to help others—especially from trying to help others enjoy spiritual growth. Growth can come by seeking humbly to be more useful tools in god's hands. Giving to others material things might help the growth of the giver, but it often injures the receiver. Is it better to help the receiver

to find ways to grow spiritual himself? Is it more far-sighted to give advice and instruction, like a wise father to a son whom he loves? Helping the poor to grow spiritually and to become givers themselves is a real road to permanent riches, including material riches. Over and over it has been demonstrated that there is wisdom in tithing.

21. Charles Grandison Finney, a great revivalist of the 19th century, taught that insofar as people are willing to live in accord with spiritual standards, economic and social troubles will diminish. After a person is spiritually born again, he or she can be twice as useful in the world. Hence the lives of Christians ought to be lived at a fever pitch like those of a rescue party in the aftermath of a disaster. In this spirit it would seem out of place to sing, "The great church victorious will be the church at rest."[29] Is this like saying "Graduate from the university so you can stop learning"? Spiritual growth does not result from rest but from research and diligence.

22. If the earth is a great classroom when considered from an eternal point of view, then are troubles and strife the examinations that test our learning skills? God gives little credit for mere attendance but scores us on how we meet the tests. Do we receive blessings in proportion to our diligent use of the talents and blessings already given to us? But the work most often neglected is the work of spiritual education. If god created the earth as a school, then what about those students who are lazy and neglectful of their lessons? Will they fail the test? Life on earth is brief. We are in this school only a few years. Why should we waste even one day? At the end of each day, can we say we have learned to radiate to all pure unlimited love and helped our neighbor to learn the joy of giving love? Brilliance of mind is not the same as beauty of character, but both yield helpful results.

23. Perhaps one of the great lessons to learn while on earth is that building our heaven is up to us. Emanuel Swedenborg wrote that we

will not be in heaven until heaven is in us. Here on earth, we can begin to receive the life and spirit of heaven within us. Swedenborg also believed that heaven is a kingdom of "uses," where everyone is challenged to his or her full potential, where contributing to the welfare of others brings happiness. Is heaven first glimpsed on the day we realize that each of us has unique and valuable gifts that are intended for the benefit of the world in which we now live? Who can find ways for scientists to research such concepts?

24. Charles Fillmore's view was that "many mansions" no longer means ethereal apartment dwellings but, according to modern theology, states of mind or of being.

25. If we view the earth as god's garden for nurturing souls, then should we follow Jesus' example of witnessing to that kingdom of god that is present on earth now? In his miracles of healing, Jesus did not say, "I will heal you after you die or when I come again." He said, "Rise up now and walk." In and through Jesus' example, people are helped to grow spiritually. Are such teachings important for showing us more of the nature of divinity? Do they instruct us in ways to become more divine and assure us that we can begin to experience heaven during this life?

26. Who are the happiest people you have ever met? If we were to write down the names of ten persons who continually bubble over with happiness, would we probably find that most are men and women who radiate love for everyone around them? Are they happy deep inside themselves because they are growing spiritually?

27. If perfection may be beyond human reach, each human only can study and strive toward such divine love. Even the saints need to work daily to maintain continuous overflowing love for friends and foe alike. But the more we love, the easier it becomes to love even more. Love given multiplies. Love hoarded disappears.

28. These sayings could well be called laws of love. If we radiate love, we receive joy, prosperity, happiness, peace and long life in return. But if we give love only to gain one of these rewards, then we have not understood love. Love professed in expectation of any reward is not authentic love. When we learn to radiate unselfish love, are we fulfilling divine purpose? Are we opening the door to heaven on earth for ourselves and others?

29. From the variety of nations on earth, would we find it more beneficial to live in a nation where many people have put great effort into spiritual growth or in a nation whose citizenry remains spiritually undeveloped and uneducated? What differences could we expect to find? From any community, select the dozen most beloved men or women. Will they be mostly god's followers? When people radiate love, love returns to them multiplied.

30. Samuel Taylor Coleridge (1772-1834) said that the truth of religion is found in the way it answers the deepest needs of a person's spirit. To put it a light-hearted way, some say that when we "get religion," even our dog or cat can see a change in us.

31. In conclusion, can readers of this book send to John Templeton Foundation suggestions for opportunities for various sciences to research additional spiritual information and spiritual progress?

CHAPTER ELEVEN

Creative Thinking
for Increasing Discoveries

1. Not infrequently one hears people make comments such as, "I'm going out of my mind" or "my mind is playing tricks on me" or "I'm losing my mind." The mind is certainly an elusive component of every human being. But it is also a most critical link between our bodies and our souls. With it we can think about our nature, other people, our bodies and our souls. We can even think about thinking; that is, we can use our minds to think about our minds. Most likely, our mind is what distinguishes our mental capacity from that of animals. Are animals at a less evolved level than humankind because they do not seem to be able to step back mentally and reflect upon themselves? Animals have instincts, some level of primitive thought and even emotion. They can build environments and communicate with each other, even with us. But as far as we can tell, animals cannot philosophize about anything.

2. Do we often feel blown by the winds of emotion? Can we become tired or irritable, frustrated or depressed? Life can seem overwhelming, or we may be beset by anxieties or fears or worries. We can suffer a sense of insecurity, or fret that we are under-appreciated or have been treated wrongly or unfairly. We can nurse grudges and criticize and argue in our minds. There is much that we know, all too well, about the harm that negative thoughts and feelings can do within our minds. Yet we have the potential to exercise great control over our

minds and to train them to be beneficial. This aspect of the training of the mind is one area where religion has great strengths of experience to offer, which can be illuminated and possibly strengthened by science.

3. As human beings, have we been given these highly developed, extremely complex, creative minds, which are capable of becoming modeled into habits of thinking, which inwardly realize and outwardly display the life and fruits of the divine spirit in which we live and breathe and have our being? Were we created for a purpose, including possibly to be helpful in the continuing and accelerating creativity? Why are we endowed with a mental capacity for broad-based creativity, including the ability to know, learn, evaluate, solve problems and improve our selves and our societies? In this way we may be created somewhat in the image and likeness of our creator. With minds searching for and receptive to divine revelations, both spiritual and natural, maybe we can be humble helpers in future progress.

4. People's minds appear capable of creative activity in the maturation of the universe, as well as the maturation of the soul. By following a path of being humble and open-minded with respect to divine reality, can we keep our minds open and receptive because we never know what opportunities await us? In this way, can the creative process in which we are engaged flow from the mind of god through our souls to our minds where creative thinking can produce creative results in the visible world and in spiritual wealth?

5. Can we see evidences of the divine effecting changes in the culture we humans create within our homes, families, schools, churches, businesses and governments? May we also be aware of spiritual growth in our own personalities? On the other hand, if we let slip our control over our thoughts, can we produce disastrous effects, much like some persons who think or feel their way psychosomatically into illness? Our

minds are powerful. They can bring on physical sickness and influence rate of recovery. If minds unconsciously can produce such results inside our bodies, imagine what, with conscious effort, they could achieve in our civilization!

6. It is a sad truth that many people have mental lives which make them appear as self-centered as little children; whereas relatively few people have yet learned to control their minds by enriching their spiritual sense and maturity so that they radiate the gifts of the spirit. For this reason, is there great opportunity to be encouraged and joyful about the prospects for the future, as people increasingly learn about the fruits of the spirit and how to nurture and cultivate them step by step toward spiritual maturity? Can persons try to begin their entry into heaven while on earth? How can we make the most of our years on earth, in developing our spiritual talents, and learning to find joy and create goodness in serving the needs of others? For example, how can each person learn in many ways to radiate love? One of the simplest ways is by beginning to practice a habit of thanksgiving. A heart full of gratitude is ready and prepared to radiate love. If, before getting up from bed each morning, for example, we learn to make a habit of saying a small prayer of thanksgiving, naming five of our blessings and miracles, then progressively over time we can discover that a new and fresh kind of radiance will come over us and we will find that it is easy to start each day with sense of happy thanksgiving which conditions us to be enthusiastic and prepares us to radiate love to others. What science experiments or statistical evidences can encourage more people to work on spiritual progress?

7. Since we have the gift of self-consciousness, should we not examine our lives from time to time to see how we are using our minds, imaginations and our will, especially to build god's kingdom through love? Practicing careful introspection is one method we can use to learn to be creative in controlling our thoughts. Each word or action

begins as a thought. We can say loving words and do loving deeds only if our minds and hearts are full of love. Is it good to stand watch over each thought that sprouts in the mind? If it is a loving thought, let us cultivate it. If it is not, can we crowd it out by filling our mind with loving thoughts? Try this experiment: Think of any person you envy or resent. Then free the mind of that poison by seeing that person as a child of god, and pray for that person's welfare as an experiment in self-discipline. The divine dwells in various ways in every human being, so it is easy to find good qualities in any person if we lovingly try. As Jesus said, we should pray for those who irritate us. Our mind is very much like a garden, fertile with good soil, water, sunlight and drainage. We, as the gardeners of our minds, can cultivate whatever thoughts we choose. Should we nourish good thoughts, weed out the bad ones and ensure that evil thinking does not overshadow and block out the radiance of the good? By years of careful thought control, your mind can become a garden of indescribable beauty. "As a man thinketh so is he."

8. For the sake of clarity and simplicity, some analysts think of each person as composed of four basic components: *god, soul, mind* and *body*. Philosophers, cosmologists, theologians and poets have used a great variety of words, synonyms and analogies to describe such distinctive realities. But the multitude of terms tends to obscure exact meanings. Of course this quartet is an oversimplification. Reality may be vastly more complex and infinite.

9. However, for the sake of simplicity, it may provide a helpful working typology. Some have considered *god* to be the infinite creator of the cosmos. If divinity is truly infinite, then how can anything exist apart from divinity? Are all other realities created reflections of the divine ground of being? Most major religions teach that each soul is immortal and can be educated. This hope always has and continues to

give us joy and enthusiasm to develop virtues. In this context, often the *mind* is conceived as a strategic link between soul and body. Mind represents our everyday capacity for thinking which is emergent within the flesh of our bodies. Mind is complex and miraculous but temporary. Often, the human *body* is defined as temporary in the sense that it does not possess a participation in the eternity of god. Is it far better to have a powerful and/or beautiful mind than a powerful and/or beautiful body, and far better still to have beauty of spirit in ways that join with the eternal divine love? Appearances seldom reveal the underlying truths. The earth appears to be flat, but actually it is round. It appears to be still, but actually it is moving in at least four directions at incredible speeds. The egg looks dead and inert until the day the bird breaks out. As Emerson said, "Things we see are out-picturing more basic realities that we do not see." The ultimate causes, forces and purposes of things are invisible. Do we usually see only a few outward manifestations, not the causes and forces themselves, but only their effects? What science research or statistical evidence can help us better discover the basic invisible spiritual realities?

10. Is our body like our house? Also, is our mind? Let us take care of it while we live in it, using our mind to help develop our soul. Can the beauty we cultivate within be the engine which can empower our minds and personalities to radiate love and joy and peace? "So within, so without," the saying goes. Why worry if our mind is feeble, if it is good enough to connect our soul with the world while we try to develop our soul? The life lived in the open seems to be only a surface reflection of the life lived in closed sessions with our divinity. Can the laws that govern the realm of soul be researched and learned, but not always in the way we learn the laws of arithmetic, physics or human logic?

11. Ramakrishna once said:

It is the mind that makes one wise or ignorant, bound or emancipated. One is holy because of his mind, one is wicked because of his mind, one is a sinner because of his mind and it is the mind that makes one vigorous. So he whose mind is always fixed on god requires no other practices, devotion or spiritual exercises.

12. Unfortunately, most of us do not possess the spiritual ability that allows total concentration on divinity. We need to work at controlling our minds and channeling our thoughts. Norman Vincent Peale's approach, which he called positive thinking, is an excellent strategy for the sort of mental discipline needed for the humble approach. Other gifted writers have provided valuable insights to ponder.

13. Ella Wheeler Wilcox (1855-1919) wrote in her poem "Attainment":

> Use all your hidden forces.
> Do not miss the purpose of this life,
> and do not wait for circumstances to mold or
> change your fate!

14. And in "You Never Can Tell," she wrote:

> You never can tell what your thoughts will do
> in bringing you hate or love,
> For thoughts are things, and their airy wings
> Are swifter than carrier doves
> They follow the law of the Universe,
> Each thing must create its kind,
> And they speed o'er the track to bring you back
> Whatever went out of your mind.

15. Marcus Bach wrote:

To dwell upon goodness is to become the recipient of all that is good. To be joyful is to attract more joyfulness. To meditate on love is to grow lovely in the inner self. To think health is to be healthy. To put life into god's love is to put god's love into your life.

16. Is there an intimate relationship between what we think and what we are? The Dhammapada scriptures, attributed to the Buddha, put it this way:

All that we are is the result of what we have thought: it is founded on our thoughts, it is made up of our thoughts, it is our thoughts. If a man speaks or acts with an evil thought, pain follows him, as the wheel follows the route of the ox that draws the carriage. . . . If a man speaks or acts with a pure thought, happiness follows him, like a shadow that never leaves him.... Hatred does not cease by hatred at any time; hatred ceases by love—this is an old rule. . . . As rain breaks through an ill-thatched house, passion will break through an unreflecting mind. . . . If one man conquer in battle a thousand times a thousand men, and another conquer himself, he is the greatest of conquerors. One's own self conquered is better than all other people conquered; not even a god could change into defeat the victory of a man who vanquished himself.

17. Why do not all people learn to benefit from controlling their own minds, which is probably the most useful tool we will ever possess? Can science research or statistical evidence help convince more people to want to govern their thoughts? Some people allow their minds to run as loose and as uncontrolled as a spilled cup of mercury. Some are not even aware that they can control their minds. Some are just too lazy. In fact, the mind is only an instrument. Each person can guide thoughts and even emotions into any paths he or she wishes. We can each learn to be the pilot of our mind. A ship without a pilot leads to disaster. So does a mind and body without a pilot. Even ordinary people wield extraordinary power in the words that leave their lips. Jesus was addressing each of us when he said:

For the words that the mouth utters come from the overflowing of the heart. A good man produces good from the store of good within himself; and an evil man from evil within produces evil. I tell you this: there is not a thoughtless word that comes from men's lips but they will have to account for it on the day of judgment. For out of your own mouth you will be acquitted; out of your own mouth you will be condemned. (Matthew 12:35–37 NEB)

18. Has divinity given each person a mind capable of creative activity as part of the ongoing complexity of the cosmos, which may include the expansion of his own soul? The creative process goes from thoughts to deeds. Our words are our thoughts crystallized. The objects we build and the deeds we accomplish emanate from our thoughts and our words.

19. Obviously, to build a house we begin with thoughts, then words, then deeds. Most good objects produced by humanity are created by this process, which starts with thoughts and then develops into words and then deeds. Nations are formed in this way, and so are sciences, as are all the organizations and institutions of human society. Even more awesome is the fact that thoughts can build not only outwardly but inwardly. By thoughts we create not only our possessions but also our personalities and our souls. By the long practice of controlling our thoughts, can each of us make ourselves the kind of person that ultimately we want to be?

20. It cannot be repeated often enough that we can learn to radiate love, but first we must practice using loving words and loving thoughts. If we keep our minds filled with good thoughts of love, giving and thanksgiving, they may spill over into our words and deeds. If we are not very careful to weed out all evil thoughts, such as envy or hate or selfishness, they, too, may overflow into our words and deeds. To produce beautiful music requires long practice, and so does the production of a beautiful mind. With practice, both come more easily. Should we beware of entertaining whatever pops into our minds? Rather, do we want to think thoughts we may be proud of and to use

them as divinely provided tools? If we really do not want to worry, then should we fill our minds with thoughts of thanksgiving, not fear? This takes self-control and practice; but the more we practice, the easier it is. What research could create enthusiasm among more young people worldwide for learning how to grow spiritually?

21. Charles Neal said in 1978:

One would think therefore that intelligent men and women, particularly prayerful ones, would be meticulous in their choice of words, speaking only those which are helpful and are constructive. And above all things, let us avoid negative and destructive words. But as we know very well, this is not what usually happens, for most people still do not really believe that they may have dominion over their own lives, and fail to exercise that dominion through the right use of their minds and have creative power. People do not seem to realize this, despite the fact that it is clearly implied again and again in our scriptures. . . . Our casual words reflect what we truly believe deep down within ourselves. They express what our thoughts have been over long periods of time and they come through spontaneously, unimpeded by deliberate and considered thought. Our so-called thoughtless words are reckoned to be true expressions of what actually is in our minds. Thus we begin to see that what some people call slips of the tongue or Freudian slips are not slips at all. Details of sickness, disharmony and woe, that every counselor and New Thought minister hears over and over again, are the products of minds that have made wrong choices in the use of ideas. Surely the cure for sickness, disharmony and woe of this kind lies in a complete change in the disciplined management of our thought process, including the very words that we utter, day by day.[30]

22. Our thoughts and words have power. Should we not discipline and manage our thoughts wisely? They can be what separate humans from the rest of creation. Can they also be what brings our unity with divinity?

CHAPTER TWELVE

Infinite Intellect: Some Questions for Fruitful Research

1. Both philosophers and scientists have always wondered about the cause of space and time. Could the cause possibly be infinite intellect? Before time and space existed, did infinite intellect exist?

2. What causes have ever been suggested for the creation of space and time other than infinite intellect, which some people have called god? If intellect is infinite, what can be separate? Does any theologian say that god has limited intellect or that other separate worshipful intellects exist?

3. Is it possibly a purpose of infinite intellect to express itself in increasingly awesome varieties of lesser intellects? Do the words *infinite intellect* convey a meaning much different from the biblical words *holy ghost*?

4. What is the intellect of an atom, a microbe, a tree or an insect? Have there been a series of smaller intellects preceding larger intellects? Does a microbe show intellect by finding food, by shaping itself and by multiplying?

5. Can humans discover larger fractions of infinite intellect? Are we rewarded when we strive to increase our own intellect or give our children better intellect? Can your intellect help others' intellects to blossom?

6. How do we account for the layer upon layer of infinite intellectual order lying hidden beneath the surface of everyday phenomena? Do we carry within us an innate sense of the infinite intellect and become inspired to think, feel and do the things that maintain harmony and productivity within us and within our environment? How can this be brought forth into conscious awareness?

7. When humans discover over a million times more information, will this be food to produce more intellect and more wisdom? Can humanity discover increasingly large fractions of infinite intellect? Have other forms of creatures unknown to humans already discovered more? If the universe visible to humans has hundreds of billions of other planets, what are the chances that intellect beyond human concepts is already comprehended by others?

8. Do egotistic humans now imagine they are the ultimate intelligence for whom the universe was created? Has more been discovered in the two centuries after 1800 than in forty thousand previous centuries? Will the next century discoveries be many times as great as the past century? Even then, will humans on one tiny planet comprehend even 1% of the vast basic creative intelligence?

9. Are materials visible to each creature only temporary out-picturing of more basic invisible realities? Are there many basic invisible realities that have attracted only small amounts of rigorous science research? Can the various sciences being eagerly developed by humans be understood as the urge to learn a bit more of infinite intellect? Were the basic invisible realities also products or aspects of infinite intellect?

10. For example, does anyone deny that love exist as a basic invisible reality? What evidences can be found of origins of love other than infinite intellect? Is love a product of humanity or is humanity a product of love? Does giving love abundantly increase your supply of love?

Is thanksgiving another example of a basic invisible reality? Has there always been a basic urge to worship and to give thanks? What new and rigorous research can be done on such basic realities?

11. Does anyone deny that creativity is a basic invisible reality? What causes the continuing increase in complexity, invention and purpose? What evidences can be found for origins of creativity other than infinite intellect? Is creativity accelerating? Why? If intelligence is manifest by accelerating creativity, are we possibly agents to accelerate this awesome creativity?

12. Among the other mysteries of human history are the basic questions: Why is there a visible universe rather than nothing? Why was humanity created? Are space, time, matter and energy a few of the creations or aspects of infinite intellect that humans are able to comprehend? Maybe there are other creations or aspects of infinite intellect that are not yet comprehensible by the human intellect. How could this possibility be explored?

13. Did intellect cause the hundreds of kinds of particles and cause them to organize into multiple varieties of atoms? Did intellect cause atoms to organize into myriad molecules? Did intellect cause molecules to organize into varieties of cells having the ability to reproduce? Did intellect cause cells to organize into plants, animals and humans? Did intellect create tools and writing and printing and universities? What comes next? Artificial intellect?

14. Does anyone deny the reality of purpose? What causes purpose? Can purpose be studied with statistics and experiments by scientists?

15. Do the beneficial principles developed by human religions give evidences of basic invisible realities and also of infinite wisdom? What science research can be devised to enhance the human store of ancient wisdom? Do minds which are humble and open become enthusiastic to discover more of infinite intellect? Is humility a help in this search?

16. How can one discover a larger fraction of infinite intellect? How does infinite intellect assist each person in playing her/her personal note in the universal symphony of life? Does discovering a larger fraction of infinite intellect in one's consciousness increase one's capacity for compassion and forgiveness? Humility? Thanksgiving? Unlimited Love? How could progress in religion increase if additional research was directed toward learning more about infinite intellect?

17. Evolution describes the processes, but does it answer the big why questions? For example, Why is there material rather than nothing? Why were you created? Why are there laws of physics? Could the big why questions be understood by us as the infinite intellect ever increasingly manifesting itself to its creatures?

18. Could discovery be accelerated if we find words with greater clarity to be used in place of some old words that instantly arouse prejudices in the minds of many great intellects? If the word *theology* is used mainly by those who study biblical concepts, could another word be found to show that discoveries of all sciences may be in reality discoveries of infinite intellect? In the minds of some scientists and other intellectuals, do the words *infinite intellect* arouse fewer unconscious prejudices than the ancient word *god* which has been so different in various civilizations? Can the word *revelation* come to mean not only god revealing himself but also humans diligently discovering more of infinite intellect? Scientists search increasingly for forms of life on other planets or beneath the ocean floor, but might search be more fruitful if not limited to our own carbon-based cellular forms of life? Can progress be enhanced by worship of multiplying mysteries more than faith in final answers?

19. Can intellectuals who reject worship of a wise king above the sky become enthusiastic participants in infinite intellect, helpers to accelerate creativity, to radiate love, to radiate thanksgiving and to research the components of infinite intellect?

20. Do we discover more about god (or infinite intellect) by faith or by search? Do we learn more by belief or by curiosity? Can we grow more by repetition or by investigation? Is habit a sign of youth or of senility? What happens to any organization or organism that stops growing? What happens if we lose our enthusiasm for finding more of the infinite intellect?

21. Can we learn to pray, "Infinite intellect invisible, I am overwhelmingly grateful and joyful for opportunities to be helpful in your accelerating creativity!"?

CHAPTER THIRTEEN

What Are Laws of Spiritual Growth?

1. We often speak about the laws of nature. Natural scientists find this legal metaphor extremely useful in discourse on the nature of the physical universe. But we need to be careful not to misunderstand it. The laws of which scientists speak are not edicts that things like atoms, photons, planets or stars consciously choose to obey. Rather these laws are invariant patterns of behavior that are expressive of the underlying nature of things. The law of gravity expresses the nature of the gravitational interaction between bodies like a planet and the Sun. Newton's laws of motion describe the way in which material bodies such as planets move in response to applied forces. Kepler's second law—the law of ellipses—describes the geometrical shape of the resulting planetary orbit as an ellipse, with the Sun located at one of the two foci of that elliptical path.

2. Because the fundamental nature of things in the universe does not appear to change, we conclude that the laws of nature do not change either, although human understanding of these patterns may often change. The patterns of behavior exhibited by physical objects appear persistent and can be succinctly described, often in the form of mathematical equations, sometimes in descriptive prose. Are these patterns of behavior the outcome of the basic nature of creation of which we are a part? They are intimately related both to the physical proper-

ties of things and the manner of their interactions. The behavioral patterns exhibited by physical objects, from the minuscule atoms in our bodies to those gigantic galaxies located billions of light years away, are manifestations of their various natures as members of the visible universe. The laws of nature express the way things appear to humans. Are they indicators of the fundamental character of the being that the creator has given to the creation?

3. Now, if there are laws of nature that appear to be expressions of the character or being of physical objects in the creation, would it not be reasonable to expect that there can be analogous laws of the spirit that are expressions of the character of spiritual realities? Once again, however, let us be careful to give a clear indication of what we mean by laws of the spirit. These laws would also be an expression of the nature of reality, but with some important differences from the laws of nature. The laws of the spirit refer to patterns of voluntary *human* behavior, not to the involuntary behavior of physical objects. A person is free to choose to act in accord with these spiritual laws or to try to defy them. This being the case, the patterns of behavior which these laws express are not uniformly exhibited by all humans at all times. Rather, they represent the ideal patterns to which human behavior may aspire. Conformity to the laws of the spirit is a free choice of responsible humans. So perhaps, to avoid misunderstandings, we should call them spiritual principles.

4. Another difference needs to be noted. As expressions of the nature of spiritual reality, the many universal laws of the spirit should be distinguished from various codes recorded by humans in particular times and places. Thus there can be differences between laws of the spirit and codes of religious laws such as those recorded by Moses, Hammurabi, Muhammad, and other ancient lawgivers. Early civilizations adopted complex and sometimes rather rigid systems of religious laws. Many of these religious teachings may have reflected basic spiri-

tual principles, but some may have reflected social and religious customs of ancient cultures. By the laws of the spirit we mean discovery of multitudes of universal principles of the unseen world that can be described and tested by extensive and rigorous examination of human behavior and other relevant data. By their fruits, you can know them. By continually and carefully researching spiritual principles, can humanity reap substantial benefits, both for the individual and for human society at large? Can this point to challenging opportunities for beneficial researches by scientists and theologians?

5. Partly for lack of clearly defined methodologies and a sufficient body of research data, is this science research for more spiritual information now about as disorganized and controversial as the natural sciences were in the millennia before Galileo? In the days of Moses or Muhammad, there was very little knowledge of the principles of physics, chemistry or biology, and little appreciation among average people of the progress and rich rewards that could be achieved through successful research in these fields. In our day, we are privileged to witness some of the fruitfulness of researches in those natural sciences.

6. Just as people of earlier times were ignorant regarding the need for research in the natural sciences, do most people today ignore needs for research about spiritual principles of human behavior? In addition to having a meager understanding and minimal agreement as to what spiritual laws are, many do not seem to recognize that the creator's intention for our education might be that we grow in our knowledge of what is good and beneficial. Should we be content with some permanent status quo, or should we be aware of the value of research, process and progress about the laws of the spirit? The spiritual dimensions of the cosmos can be dynamic, changing and ceaselessly developing. Has the time come for us to concentrate more resources on the kind of investigations which may enable us to understand better the patterns and

principles for the attainment of spiritual growth and development? Should not ceaseless seeking be a part of the growth of souls as well as minds? Should it not be possible through research and cooperative reflection to reach some agreements on some principles of the spirit and benefits from studying such principles? Can this field of research soon become as bounteously fruitful as the natural sciences were in the 19th and 20th centuries?

7. Therefore, if fruitful advance is to take place, should research into many laws of the spirit be undertaken by exceptionally competent persons who are rigorously trained in many fields of science: physical, psychological, medical, behavioral and economic? Already, some leaders in exact sciences are beginning to speak and write about their religious perspectives and to perform research on questions regarding the helpfulness of spiritual principles to human behavior. Can research help to clarify or verify some of the laws of spirit and their benefits?

8. The goal of investigations can be increased understanding concerning the ideal patterns of human behavior. Can research demonstrate what happens when human behavior conforms to divine laws? Although our research need not be confined to examination of revered texts alone, the scriptures can provide a good place to begin. It is not immediately apparent exactly how various laws of the spirit could be accurately described, tested and utilized. Neither can we predict what laws will be discovered by future generations of scientists sifting data for evidences of the effects of the unseen. Similarly, it would have been impossible five hundred years ago to predict anything of the laws of thermodynamics or electronics or nuclear physics, let alone the devising of experiments to test and establish them as laws. The difficulties of bringing to light, of describing and testing the laws of the spirit, can seem as baffling now as those which physicists and chemists faced as recently as 1800 or those faced by medical scientists in 1900.

9. Researching and teaching spiritual principles may benefit humanity in even greater measure than did, for example, the laws of chemistry. Matthew Arnold thought that the decreasing influence of the Bible in the 19th century could be reversed if the ideals and hopes and laws expressed in the poetic and allegorical language of the scriptures could be explored experimentally. He hoped that dogmatic theology could be improved by empirical theology or experimental theology. If people could understand religious principles in their own everyday language rather than in ancient metaphors, he thought people might take them more seriously. Likewise, if we could research more about the beneficial effects of spiritual laws operating in the 21st century rather than just reading about their effects in ancient Israel, might we become more enthusiastic to live our lives in closer harmony with spiritual realities?

10. Is it possible that there are some spiritual principles on which all major religions already agree? Would we expect that to be the case? For example, ancient Hindus taught that hate is never overcome by hate, but hate can be overcome by love. Does any religion now disagree? Such agreements might be useful in providing some starting points for further inquiry, experimental testing and the better formulation of laws of the spirit.

11. Is it necessary, however, or even desirable, that everyone should agree entirely on any fixed code or list of laws? Neither were natural scientists ever in absolute agreement about laws of nature. Some diversity of judgment and opinion can often be beneficial because disagreement sometimes induces progress. Perhaps the amazing acceleration of scientific discovery and progress in the 20th century is due in part to increasing diversity and constructive rivalry in the domains of the sciences. It would never be wise for any world government to codify a list of laws of science or laws of spirit, either, because progress and advance in research might be severely discouraged.

12. Would more benefits result in the domain of the spirit if each individual were to draw up her own personal list of the laws governing spiritual matters? Of course, a person would be well advised first to study books and articles of scientists engaged in investigating possible laws of the spirit. However, only when we understand and claim as our own some actual spiritual principles can we begin to build our own concept of divine reality. What could be more uplifting than for each person to write in her mind and heart, as well as on paper, the various laws by which one ought to live? She could measure her spiritual growth if every year she revised and rewrote her own personal lists of laws. How beneficial it would be if schools devoted a few minutes a day to help pupils study great spiritual principles as they are brought to light and then clarified and tested by great scientists. Then each person could improve her own written list. The supreme moments in the life of each of us occur whenever we grasp a new inspiring truth and appropriate it so that it revitalizes our personality and becomes an inspiration for our life.

13. When any field of research is begun, no one can possibly predict what may eventually be discovered. Astronomers before Copernicus could not have predicted or even imagined the galaxies or supernovas or pulsars that we are now aware of. In the same way, no one can yet say what laws of the spirit will be formulated and eventually verified. But to give some idea of laws of the spirit which might be researched, here are a few examples taken mostly from the wisdom of the centuries expressed by the world's major religions. Analogues to the conclusions of modern science, these represent distillations of much systematic reflection and research on authentic human experience.

    i) Religions generally agree that "as a person thinks, so is that person." If this is an authentic and demonstrable spiritual law and if it can be taught convincingly, especially to young people, it might be the basis for new generations much more disciplined in the control and management of their minds and lives than current generations.

ii) "Happiness comes from spiritual wealth, not material wealth." Happiness is always a by-product, never a product. Happiness comes from giving, not getting. If we pursue happiness for ourselves, it will always elude us. If we strive to bring happiness to others, we cannot stop it from coming to us also. The more we try to give it away, the more it comes back to us multiplied. If we try to grasp happiness, it always escapes us; if we try to hand it out to others, it sticks to our hands like glue.

iii) "The more love we give away, the more we have left." The laws of love differ from the laws of arithmetic. Love hoarded dwindles, but love given grows. If we give all our love, we will have more left than the person who tries to keep some in reserve. Giving love, not receiving, is important; but when we give with no thought of receiving, we automatically and inescapably receive abundantly. The experience of heaven is a by-product of love. When we say "I love you," we mean that "a little of god's love flows from me to you." But, thereby, we do not love less, but more. For in flowing the quantity is magnified. God's love is infinite, and is directed equally to each person, but it seems to gain intensity when directed to those who need it the most. This is the wonder and mystery of it, that when we love god we get an enormous increase in the quantity of love flowing through us to others.

iv) "It is better to give than to receive." Giving is a sign of personal and spiritual maturity. There are few diseases so childish and so deadly as the "gimmies," a disease that tends to isolate us from friends and from god and to shrink the soul. The secret of success is giving, not getting. To get joy we must give it and to keep joy we must scatter it. The greatest charity is to help a person change from being a receiver to being a giver.

v) "Loneliness is the punishment for those who want to get, not give." Helping others is the cure for loneliness. If we feel lonely, we are probably self-centered. If we feel unloved, we are probably unloving. If we love only ourselves, we may be almost the only person who loves us. Whatever we give out, we get back.

vi) "Thanksgiving opens the door to spiritual growth." If there is any day in our lives which is not thanksgiving day, then we are not fully alive. Counting our blessings attracts blessings. Counting our blessings each morning will launch a day full of blessings. Thanksgiving brings god's bounty. From gratitude comes riches—from complaints, poverty. Thankfulness opens the door to happiness. Thanksgiving causes more giving. Thanksgiving puts our mind in tune with the Infinite. Continual gratitude dissolves our worries.

vii) "To be forgiven, we must first forgive." Forgiving brings forgiveness. Failure to forgive creates a greater hell for the unforgiver than for the unforgiven. In 1999 numerous scientists began research on how to forgive and on world benefits from forgiving.

viii) When Jesus was asked what is the greatest law, he said:

> Thou shalt love the Lord thy God with all thy heart, and with all thy soul, and with all thy mind. This is the first and great commandment. And the second is like unto it, Thou shalt love they neighbor as thyself. On these two commandments hang all the law and the prophets (Matthew 22:37–40 KJV).

This can be researched as a basic law of the spirit. A person who applies this law often finds her life revolutionized. Opening our hearts allows god's love to flow through us like a mighty river. If we love as god loves us, we learn to love every person without any exception. The happiest people on earth seem to be those who give love wholeheartedly always.

ix) "Surrender to god brings freedom." It is in dying to our selfish selves (humility) that we are born to eternal life.

x) "A false witness shall not be unpunished, and he that speaketh lies shall not escape" (Proverbs 19:1 KJV). Do we not have daily evidence of this in the confirmation of the proverb "Honesty is the best policy"? Honesty leads to prosperity. Those who are trustworthy are the ones entrusted with great blessings. Even in the lives of nations this law of the spirit is manifest, for any nation whose people are steadfast in authentic religion, fair play, hard work, thrift, personal initiative and trustworthiness will automatically grow in prosperity also.

14. More and more manpower and resources are being devoted to the forces of nature—discovering, proving, understanding, using and teaching about these forces. But almost everyone agrees that one of the greatest forces on earth is *love*. Should churches finance continuing research into this force of love? Should schools offer courses for credit (with homework, tests and grades) on the influences of love? The real wealth of a nation does not come from mineral resources but from the way it develops and harnesses the lovepower in the minds and hearts of its people.

15. In the Christian scriptures several accounts of this force of love are presented very vividly and clearly:

Dear friends, let us love one another, because love is from God. Everyone who loves is a child of God and knows God, but the unloving know nothing of God. For God is love; . . . If God thus loved us, dear friends, we in turn are bound to love one another. Though God has never been seen by any man, God himself dwells in us if we love one another; his love is brought to perfection within us.

God is love; he who dwells in love is dwelling in God, and God in him. This is for us the perfection of love. . . . There is no room for fear in love; perfect love banishes fear. For fear brings with it the pains of judgment, and anyone who is afraid has not attained to love in its perfection. We love because he loved us first. But if a man says, 'I love God', while hating his brother, he is a liar. If he does not love the brother whom he has seen, it cannot be that he loves God whom he has not seen. And indeed this command comes to us from Christ himself: that he who loves God must also love his brother. (1 John 4:7–21 NEB)

If you love only those who love you, what credit is that to you? Even sinners love those who love them. Again, if you do good only to those who do good to you, what credit is that to you? Even sinners do as much. And if you lend only where you expect to be repaid, what credit is that to you? Even sinners lend to each other to be repaid in full. But you must love your enemies and do good; and lend without expecting any return; and you will have a rich reward; you will be sons of the Most High, because he himself is kind to the ungrateful and wicked. Be compassionate as your Father is compassionate.

Pass no judgment, and you will not be judged; do not condemn, and you will not be condemned; acquit, and you will be acquitted; give, and gifts will be given you. Good measure, pressed down, shaken together, and running over, will be poured into your lap; for whatever measure you deal out to others will be dealt to you in return. (Luke 6:32–38 NEB)

And now I will show you the best way of all.

I may speak in tongues of men or of angels, but if I am without love, I am a sounding gong or a clanging cymbal. I may have the gift of prophecy, and know every hidden truth; I may have faith strong enough to move mountains; but if I have no love, I am nothing. I may dole out all I possess, or even give my body to be burnt, but if I have no love, I am none the better.

Love is patient; love is kind and envies no one. Love is never boastful, nor conceited, nor rude; never selfish, not quick to take offence. Love keeps no score of wrongs; does not gloat over the other men's sins, but delights in the truth. There is nothing love cannot face; there is no limit to its faith, its hope, and its endurance.

Love never comes to an end. But if there are prophecies, they will be done away with; if tongues, they will fall silent; and if knowledge, it will be done away with. For we know only imperfectly, and we prophesy imperfectly; but once perfection comes, all imperfect things will be done away with. When I was a child, I used to talk like a child, and see things as a child does, and think like a child; but now that I have become an adult, I have finished with all childish ways. Now we see only reflections in a mirror, mere riddles, but then we shall be seeing face to face. Now I can know only imperfectly; but then I shall know just as fully as I am myself known. As it is, these remain: faith, hope and love, the three of them; and the greatest of them is love. (1 Corinthians 12:3–13:13 NEB)

16. As can be seen in these few passages from the Christian scriptures, and in ancient scriptures of other religions, many psychospiritual truths might be discovered by researching these age-old maxims about love. Maybe we will discover that love is indeed the basic force in the spiritual world. Could Dante have been correct when he said, "It is love which moves the sun and stars"? Can both theologians and scientists be enthusiastic to convince skeptics by many various experiments and by collecting many statistics to test repeatedly worldwide many such spiritual laws?

17. Are our prayers answered? On earth we may never know the reason why many are. Is it an evidence of god's unlimited and undeserved love? Divine love is its own ultimate reason. What is our response? Should it not be an overwhelming feeling of gratitude and desire to grow spiritually?

18. Love of god comes first and makes it easier to love in other ways. If we want our enemy to see only our good qualities and not our flaws, then should we not set the example by looking first for the good qualities of the other? That person, too, is a child of god. God loves us both even though neither of us is yet perfect. Above all, should we not only radiate love but also help others to become alive with love? Can schoolchildren be taught some of the laws of the spirit rather than having to learn them slowly through sufferings in later life?

19. Throughout this discussion of the humble approach, we have been calling for and encouraging the expression of the highest and noblest qualities of the human spirit. We have been calling for rigorous research to clarify and often verify more and more spiritual principles. Have we been asking too much? Is this plea for the humble approach too unrealistic to be achieved? Well, like any quest in sciences, can answers be achieved by rigorous and repeated experiments? Human potential can be far greater than most of us realize.

20. What are we? Are we no more than creatures constituted by the possession of bodies and minds? Bodies and minds may be only our tools. To the question Who are we in ourselves? most religions answer that your real self may be your soul. Most people go to school for twelve years or more just to educate the mind, which lives only briefly. Can we not discover equally effective methods to educate the soul for eternity?

21. Two thousand years ago more time was devoted to spiritual education than to mental education. The same was true as recently as 1800.

Many famous universities were founded by ministers or religious groups to train more persons for ministry or for spiritual learning. But in the latest two centuries, have we increased mental education enormously, so that now over twenty times as many hours may be spent on mental as on spiritual improvement? No wonder the world seems out of joint. Let us not work less on mental education, but could we not expect both children and adults to study at least seven hours a week for spiritual growth? The results might be rewarding beyond our most optimistic dreams.

22. It is not surprising that our world has problems. Have many churches become no longer relevant because so little planning is devoted to spiritual education and so little time is actually set aside for it? If we tried to teach chemistry by such methods, there would be very few able chemists and few new discoveries in chemistry. Should schools include in the curriculum courses in ethics, philanthropy, character building, self-denial techniques, joy of giving, disciplined thinking and freedom from envy? To say that lessons learned from major religious should not be included in university studies because the spiritual cannot be seen or accurately measured seems as questionable as saying that love should not be studied because it cannot be weighed on a bathroom scale.

23. Do new teaching methods need to be tried? In addition to using only books and traditional classrooms exclusively, perhaps we could teach more effectively through newspapers, comics, radio, television, etc. Should more church teachers try to identify and warn against movies, magazines and plays which are harmful? Could new techniques such as programmed learning and programmed textbooks and participation in charities be adapted to teach spiritual growth more efficiently at various ages, both in daily schools and Sunday schools?

24. Animals rely on instinct, so their mental development is limited. Many homes and many schools may not go much beyond instinct in their methods for teaching spiritual growth. For rational humans,

should education be far more than merely a drawing out of what is somehow already embedded in the child as if by instinct?

25. By learning humility, can we expand our concepts and find that the purpose of life on earth is vastly deeper than previously imagined or that human spiritual potential can be more vast than any human can grasp? Diligently, each child of god should seek to find and serve the creator's purposes, but none should be so egotistical as to think that he or she comprehends the infinite mind of divinity.

26. As we become more and more humble, we can learn more about divinity. Let us recall once more that humankind is able to observe only a tiny part of reality and that our observations often can be misleading because we are prone to be self-centered.

27. Scientists have steadily modified and clarified their concepts of the universe and the laws of nature. Both the vastness and the intricacy of the physical universe stretch our imaginations and beckon us to look beyond what is visible, toward the great ocean of realities not visible. What can be seen calls us to consider the reality of a vastly greater Unseen. Mankind's observational abilities are very limited, and so are our mental abilities. Should we not focus our lives more on the unseen realities and not only on the fleeting appearances? Should we not kneel down in humility and worship the awesome, infinite, omniscient, eternal creator?

28. Is god limited to one new species on one little planet? Or is god infinite and eternal? Why then do so many people think of god as resembling a person? Instead, is it more fruitful to think of god as the basic invisible realities, which are creating everything visible and much more? Should sciences research the basic invisible realities, thereby gaining more spiritual information?

29. Is every person's concept of god too small? Through humility can we begin to get into true perspective the infinity of god? This is the

humble approach. Are we ready to begin research into a humble, ever-growing theology which can never become obsolete? Would this be a theology centered upon serving divine purposes and not focused upon our own little selves?

30. In conclusion, the eighty-seven-year-old author invites each reader to send suggestions for improvements to: John Templeton Foundation, Five Radnor Corporate Center, Suite 100, 100 Matsonford Road, Radnor, PA 19087. Most of that foundation's donations go to many entrepreneurs trying various methods to rescue all religions from obsolescence, especially by science research, to supplement the wonderfully beneficial ancient scriptures. Continual improvements and researches are needed to increase the possibility that humanity may benefit from over 100 fold more spiritual information, hopefully within just the 21st century.

Notes

ABBREVIATIONS

KJV   King James Version

NASB   New American Standard Bible

NEB   New English Bible

RSV   Revised Standard Version

1. Carl Sagan, *The Dragons of Eden: Speculations on the Evolution of Human Intelligence* (New York: Ballantine Books, 1989).
2. Vannevar Bush, "Science Pauses," *Fortune* (May 1965).
3. Ralph Waldo Trine, *In Tune with the Infinite: Fullness of Peace, Power, and Plenty* (Wellingborough: Thorsons Publishers, 1995).
4. Theodore Parker, *The Transient and the Permanent in Christianity*, 1841.
5. Arend van Leeuwin, *Christianity in World History: The Meeting of the Faiths of East and West* (London: Edinburgh House Press, 1964).
6. Huston Smith, *Empiricism: Scientific and Religious*, 1964.
7. Malcolm Muggeridge, *Something Beautiful for God: Mother Teresa of Calcutta* (San Francisco: Harper & Row, 1986).
8. Bush, "Science Pauses."
9. Marceline Bradford, "The Downfall of Communism," *The Freeman* (May 1962).

10. Harold K. Schilling, *What Is the Future of Man?* 1971.

11. Ibid.

12. Sir Bernard Lovell, *In the Center of Immensities* (New York: Harper & Row, 1978).

13. Ibid.

14. Thomas Carlyle, *Sartor Resartus,* 1838.

15. Lincoln Barnett, *The Universe and Dr. Einstein* (New York: New American Library, 1957).

16. Henry Drummond, *Natural Law in the Spiritual World* (London: Hodder & Stoughton, 1883).

17. Trine, *In Tune with the Infinite.*

18. Lovell, *In the Center of Immensities.*

19. *New York Times,* March 5, 1970.

20. Ralph Wendell Burhoe, ed., *Science and Human Values,* 1971.

21. Sagan, *Dragons of Eden.*

22. Drummond, *Natural Law in the Spiritual World.*

23. Henry Margenau, *Truth in Science and Religion,* 1960.

24. N. Max Wildiers, *An Introduction to Teilhard de Chardin* (New York: Harper & Row, 1968).

25. Ralph Waldo Trine, *What All the World's A'seeking: or The Vital Law of True Life, True Greatness, Power and Happiness* (Kessinger Publishing Co., 1942).

26. Emil Brunner, *The Divine Imperative* (New York: Macmillan, 1932).

27. Charles Neal, sermon at Unity Church, Miami, 1976.

28. Ralph Waldo Trine, *My Philosophy and My Religion,* 1896.

29. Samuel J. Stone, "The Church's One Foundation," 1949 Hymnal (New York: Church Publishing, 1985).

30. Charles Neal, sermon at Unity Church, Miami, 1978.

Ninety-two Questions on Humility in Theology and Science

SEPTEMBER 23, 1999

HUMILITY IN THEOLOGY

The Humble Approach in Theology and Science: Ninety-two questions by Sir John Templeton on methods to encourage over 100 fold increase in new additional spiritual information, especially through science research, to supplement the wonderful ancient scriptures.

Hoping to stimulate pondering and research by people of diverse cultures, a few of the following humility questions are repeated but in diverse wording.

Sir John Templeton humbly begs each reader to send suggestions for additions, deletions and revisions and to suggest examples of science research which has been or could be done on any of these questions, please.

Subjects for either increasing science research or for probability reasoning or for debate:

1. Maybe in only a century or two, can humans discover over one hundred times more spiritual information? For example, in only the 20th century, information has increased over 100 fold in electronics, medicine, etc. by science research.

2. Can total information continue to double each three years, so in thirty years one thousand times as much will be available and in sixty years a million times as much?

171

3. If things visible to humans only one millennium ago are only a tiny part of what has since been discovered, does this indicate that things visible are only a few temporary outward manifestations of fundamental reality?

4. Maybe no human has yet known even 1% of unlimited mind, which some call God. Maybe after humans gain one hundred times as much spiritual information, will we still know only 1% of reality?

5. If human information has multiplied over 100 fold in only two centuries, will that progress accelerate, so in year 2200 information can be over ten thousand times as great as 1800?

6. Can science research increase over 100 fold earthlings' information about reality, timeless and limitless, which some call God?

7. What evidence indicates that progress will continue to accelerate? In what areas are there evidences that creativity is accelerating? How can we help?

8. Is it likely that by accelerating progress, over half of what is taught as science today will become obsolete in only one century?

9. Is science research, which has flourished for only the latest 1% of 1% of human history, still in its infancy? In less than four centuries have human perceptions expanded over 100 fold?

10. Will accelerating discoveries continue to reveal multitudes of new mysteries?

11. What evidence indicates that the invisible can be over one hundred times larger and more varied than the visible?

12. Is the visible only a tiny, temporary manifestation of reality? Does 99% of science study not reality but human perceptions of reality? Do multiplying discoveries indicate that reality is more basic, complex and vast than things tangible or visible?

13. Now that sciences have shown that realities can be vastly more numerous than materials only, is it egotistical to cling to the idea that reality means visible and tangible materials?

14. Do the discoveries by science just since Galileo about realities not previously comprehended by humans resemble the discoveries about realities that followed the development of eyes by the first creature?

15. Are we egotistical to ignore the mathematicians, who are recently suggesting that reality can have as many as eleven dimensions rather than

the three dimensions plus time, which were familiar to the prophets and to Isaac Newton and Albert Einstein?

16. When billions of dollars are spent searching for life elsewhere in the cosmos, is it egotistical to think that intelligencies cannot exist unless they are comprehensible by us? Does our tiny comprehension cause us to think egotistically that we are not possibly swimming in a multitude of other intelligences? What are the chances that varieties of creatures already exist not yet comprehensible by us, even in our own vicinity?

17. Would we benefit by redefining reality to mean fundamentals instead of appearances? Can scientists study reality or only those few human perceptions of reality?

18. If we do not understand why matter exists or light or gravity, could that mean that reality is vastly more complex than humans yet comprehend, just as our ancestors did not comprehend television, germs, atoms or galaxies?

19. Could living creatures on earth only ten million years ago conceive of present human intelligence? Has recent science research already taught humans that reality is over one hundred times more complex and vast than humans perceived just two centuries ago?

20. In the next two centuries can human perception of reality be multiplied over 100 fold more? Is there evidence that human perceptions of reality are accelerating? Why? How?

21. Can human perceptions of reality be as meager as a clam's perceptions of humans?

22. Is it egotistical to think that what humans cannot yet perceive or measure is not real? Is egotism a common failing that has always caused many species to think that reality and intelligence are limited to what that species can conceive? Do most sciences serve to enlarge human perception of basic reality?

23. If science can study only human perceptions rather than reality, should we use the word *reality* to mean the total of appearances plus fundamentals?

24. Should we use the word *God* to mean something less that totality?

25. If God means totality, then what can be separate from God? Or do we want the word God to mean only part of the whole, somewhat like a king can live separate from his subjects?

26. If sciences try to study total reality, then are sciences methods for discovering more about God? Can the word *God* be defined as "basic reality"?

27. Do atheists believe there is no king, or do they believe there are no fundamentals behind the appearances, which are often shown to be fleeting or partial? Could an egotistical ocean wave claim there is no ocean?

28. Does humility help humans to comprehend that humans are only tiny, temporary parts of reality, parts of a limitless, timeless Creator whom some call God?

29. Is it possible that research in genetics or other sciences can accelerate the progress of human intelligence?

30. Now that cosmology has convinced us that our sun is only one of more than a billion billion other stars, can we still egotistically imagine ourselves to be the ultimate purpose of the cosmos?

31. If each branch of science is showing that creation is vastly wider and more complex than comprehended two millennia ago or even just one century ago, does this reveal a vastly more worshipful Creator?

32. Can human concepts of God expand even more rapidly than science reveals reality?

33. Is all science research further information about the nature and vastness of God?

34. If God is not smaller than all of reality, then are most sciences discovering more about God? Are such sciences methods of theology to be welcomed by every person seeking God?

35. Can all the wonderfully beneficial ancient scriptures be supplemented over 100 fold partly by science research for spiritual information and verification?

36. If the word *reality* no longer means a small land area on one planet, is it egotistical to think that reality cannot be vastly greater than now comprehended? If ancient peoples could imagine God usually as a spirit separate from reality, are we now egotistical to think that God can be in any way smaller or more limited than total reality?

37. Are scientists egotistical if they think that love and prayer and worship may not be a greater part of reality than visible materials?

38. Can all religions learn to be so humble as to be enthusiastic rather than resistant to new spiritual information, especially through science research, to supplement the wonderful ancient scriptures? Can most scientists become humble enough not to limit themselves to things visible or tangible but also to include various research about vastly greater spiritual realities in which we live and move and have our being?

39. Were many major religions held back by an unconscious concept that God is somehow separate from reality, a sort of wise old king?

40. Have human concepts of God always been too small? Or too anthropomorphic?

41. Has human ego caused people to imagine a God in human terms?

42. Is God larger than a single race or planet? What is the increasing evidence?

43. What additional evidence has been found that God may be timeless and unlimited? Omnipresent? Increasingly creative?

44. Will this comprehension of a larger, greater Creator continue? Why will comprehension continue to speed up?

45. Can each species think the universe was very finely tuned to produce that species because its perceptions are limited to only those parts of reality which affect that species, just as the anthropic principle might mislead humans to think egotistically that the universe was designed for a single species on one tiny planet? Is it likely that earthlings are the ultimate?

46. Is human consciousness only a tiny, recent manifestation of a vast creative consciousness which could be called God?

47. Should we be enthusiastic and diligent to discover more about God?

48. Should this cause us to worship a God even more awesome than comprehended by the ancients? Why would anyone prefer to worship a God who can be described in human terms rather than a God who is unlimited and timeless?

49. Should we listen carefully, thoughtfully and gratefully to everyone's concepts of God and God's purpose for humanity?

50. By devoting one-tenth of all science research funding to the discovery of new spiritual information, can the benefits be even greater than from all

other science research? Maybe science research for spiritual information should be over one-tenth of all research, which now exceeds one billion dollars daily.

51. Is it egotistical to think that humans can ever comprehend all of reality or of God or of his nature or of his methods or purposes?

52. Do we now comprehend over one hundred times as much about God's creativity as humans understood just one thousand years ago?

53. Is God the only reality?

54. Can anything ever be separate from God? What are the advantages of perceiving God to be separate from basic reality?

55. Is God all of you and you a tiny part of him?

56. Does humility theology mean more questions than answers?

57. Should all religions teach "how little we know and how eager to learn"?

58. Are there some laws from the great religions for happy and fruitful life which can be tested by science research and studied and researched in schools worldwide?

59. If humility is the mother of invention, could progress accelerate if religions encouraged enthusiasm for research more than creed, ritual, bureaucracy or authority? Should humility ask for evidences and research to supplement or clarify belief or faith?

60. Is creativity reduced by excessive bureaucracy but accelerated by open minds and by free competition?

61. For accelerating creativity, do we need dogma and ritual or humble, searching, open minds? Is God's creativity accelerating, and can we become helpers in this acceleration?

62. Is the ability of humans yet to understand God just as tiny as the ability of a clam to understand the ocean, of which it is a creature?

63. If a wave is a tiny temporary manifestation of the ocean of which it is a part, does that resemble our relation to God?

64. What is the evidence that free and loving competition may be part of God's method for progress, productivity, prosperity and spiritual maturity for his children?

65. Are there multiplying evidences of purpose in the universe and in creativity?

66. In the latest one-millionth of time, have humans been created on purpose for purpose? Or for pleasure?

67. What evidence is there that God lives in you and you in him?

68. Can you be an expression or agent of God in love and creativity?

69. To enhance human comprehension of God, should science research examine benefits of limitless love, purpose and accelerating creativity?

70. Would we enhance our worship of God by using that word to mean limitless, timeless, total reality instead of merely a separate humanlike superior king as often pictured in ancient scriptures of the chosen tribe of Abraham?

71. Why were we created? Could one purpose be for us to help in God's accelerating creativity? How can we learn to be helpers in God's purposes?

72. How can we discover more about God's purposes? What is the purpose for humans and for human purpose?

73. Always, humans have wondered why they were created. Could a possible purpose be to help accelerate God's creativity, similar in some tiny ways to the ways humans recently create intelligent computers?

74. Is trying to help in God's creativity processes a way to express our worship and thankfulness?

75. How is the search for increasing comprehension of God helped by the New Testament statements, *God is love and he who dwells in love dwells in God and God in him.* And *With God were all things made and without Him was not anything made that was made?*

76. Can prayer, worship and service to others help each of us to discover more of the nature of God?

77. Is it likely that on the planets of over one hundred billion stars in our galaxy and one hundred billion other galaxies there are manifestations of God's creativity not yet imagined by earthlings and maybe more advanced than we?

78. Is it possible to give too much divine love? What English words can separate divine love from hormone love and filial love? How can we distinguish giving too many goods or instructions (which can retard maturity) from divine love, which helps the receiver to gain the joy of giving? If

instead of greeting people with the words, "How are you?" we began to say "God loves you and so do I," what could be the benefits?

79. What evidence indicates that heaven on earth can be the result of prayer, worship, usefulness and giving, forgiving and thanksgiving and unlimited love?

80. What is the evidence that enthusiasm for worship can increase as we learn more of the timeless, limitless, omnipresent God?

81. How large is your God? Is he only a wise Father? Is he God of a single tribe or race or planet? Is he somehow separate from reality, or is he the only reality? Besides searching for intelligencies in the vast cosmos, should we search for intelligencies around us and within us not yet comprehensible by us?

82. Could even atheists, who deny the reality of a personal God, begin to worship fundamental reality or unlimited mind or unlimited love?

83. If dinosaurs were egotistical, could they have thought of themselves as the ultimate purpose of the universe?

84. If the first microbes on earth more than a billion years ago were egotistical, could they have thought of themselves as the ultimate purpose of the universe? If one of the more than four hundred varieties of microbes, which help us digest our food, were egotistical, could they now think of themselves as the ultimate purpose of the universe because they are unable to comprehend more complex or intelligent creatures?

85. In what ways can free competition of diverse spiritual concepts accelerate progress in religion, ideas and human welfare?

86. Can new information from science research reduce conflict between religions?

87. Have all wars that were called religious really been manifestations of egotism where one tribe or bureaucracy imagined itself to possess the total truth and, therefore, should either convert or kill any persons suggesting a different concept?

88. Could religious wars vanish if 90% of spiritual information came from science research, which is verifiable worldwide? Can the mottos of religions become "How little we yet know, how eager to search"?

89. Should universities and schools that teach sciences of visible materials also teach sciences of unlimited love and purpose and ethics? By statistics and questionnaires, can scientists research realities such as love and purpose and worship?

90. Can some universities encourage and train some students to choose careers in humility theology research?

91. Is agape love a product of the human mind, or can human minds be a product of pure, limitless, timeless love, which some call God?

92. Are multiplying mysteries even more awesome and worshipful than a king above the sky of one planet? Although most of the world's religious people will now say, if asked, that their God is limitless, do most atheists think that word means some concept smaller or separate?

John Templeton Foundation Purpose Clause 1998

PURPOSES OF THE JOHN TEMPLETON FOUNDATION

I. *Purposes.* The Foundation is incorporated under the Tennessee Nonprofit Corporation Act, as amended, for exclusively charitable, scientific, educational, literary and religious purposes within the meaning of Section 501(c)(3) of the Internal Revenue Code of 1986, as amended (the "Code") (any reference in this Charter or the Foundation's Bylaws to any section of the Internal Revenue Code shall include the corresponding provision of any future tax code or law). The purposes of the Foundation shall be limited to the activities set forth in the following paragraphs A, B and C, and all such activities are subject to the Limitations on Expenditures after the Death of the Founder as set forth in article VI:

A. *Humility-in-Theology.* Advancing Humility-in-Theology, which is defined as helping spiritual information to multiply over 100 fold about every two centuries, especially by encouraging people of all religions to become enthusiastic (rather than resistant) to new additional spiritual information, especially through science research, to supplement the wonderful ancient scriptures. Humility-in-Theology includes: (i) supporting or creating science research and science research organizations for finding or publicizing new spiritual information, including, for example, research methods and instruments to test and measure basic forces and realities, such as love, prayer, purpose, altruism, creativity, thanksgiving and other spiritual forces as described in more detail in *Worldwide Laws of Life* (Templeton Foundation Press, 1997)(to be republished under the title *Keys to Productive Living: Spiritual Principles of World Religions)*; (ii) encouraging humility that comprehension of total reality can multiply over 100 fold, thereby expanding comprehension of the creator's accelerating creativity, in which humans may help; (iii) encouraging research on non-material realities not yet widely researched by scientists, or research on the possibilities that diverse intelligences may have been created that are not yet easily recognizable by humans; and (iv) encouraging scientists, either individually or as a discipline or profession, to have the humility to recognize the possible existence of such spiritual forces, even though they may not yet be easily measured, so that more scientists may apply their skills to the development of productive research.

1. *Primary Descriptions of Humility-in-Theology.* For clarification of the term Humility-in-Theology, twelve books and essays authored or co-authored by John M. Templeton (the "Founder") are listed below, and copies, in their current form, are attached to this Charter.

    a. *The Humble Approach*, a book by John Marks Templeton, first edition published by Seabury Press in 1982, second edition published by Continuum Publishing Company in 1995, and scheduled to be published in 2000 with the title *Possibilities for Over One Hundredfold More Spiritual Information: The Humble Approach in Theology and Science;*

    b. *The God Who Would Be Known*, a book by John Marks Templeton and Robert L. Herrmann published by Harper & Row in 1989;

    c. "The Theology of Humility," a signed and notarized essay by John Marks Templeton dated March 1, 1990, as revised on October 6, 1995;

    d. "Humility Theology Questions—Is It Limiting or Egotistical to Think?" a signed and notarized essay by John Marks Templeton dated June 25, 1993;

e. "Humility Theology Information Center—A Limited Explanation," a signed and notarized essay by John Marks Templeton dated June 25, 1993;

f. "April 1993 Supplementary Comments About Humility Theology," a signed and notarized essay by John Marks Templeton dated August 23, 1993;

g. Is God the Only Reality?, a book by John Marks Templeton and Robert L. Herrmann published by Continuum Publishing Company in 1994, and scheduled to be revised in 1999;

h. "Like a Wave on the Ocean," a signed and notarized essay by John Marks Templeton dated July 21, 1995;

i. "A Statement on Humility Theology," an essay edited, signed and notarized by John Marks Templeton dated December 29, 1995;

j. "Understanding: Acceleration in Spiritual Information," a signed and notarized essay by John Marks Templeton, which he delivered as a speech at the 1995 Unity Conference held in the United Kingdom;

k. "Humility Theology," a signed and notarized essay by John Marks Templeton dated December 26, 1997; and

l. "Humility in Theology—The Humble Approach in Theology and Science" —92 Questions by John M. Templeton dated September 24, 1998.

2. *Founder's Intentions.* The major intentions of the Founder are: (i) to encourage new spiritual information and spiritual research to increase as rapidly as medical information has in the 20th century; (ii) to encourage the world to spend at least one-tenth as much resources on research for new spiritual information as the world spends on all science research; and (iii) to encourage the idea that less than 1% of spiritual reality is yet known by humans, just as less than 1% of the cosmos was known before Nicholas Copernicus. For spiritual wealth it seems far more cost-effective to search for supplementary spiritual information rather than to pay for more study of the wonderful ancient scriptures. Accordingly, the

Founder wants the Foundation to encourage cooperation between entrepreneurs and religious leaders, who are trying various ways to rescue religions of all kinds from obsolescence, and pay for proposals for helping to multiply over 100 fold mankind's spiritual wealth (instead of donating to charities or encouraging ideas already widely popular and widely financed by governments, religious organizations and others). The Founder intends for new spiritual information and spiritual research to be that kind of scholarly, open-minded inquiry that usually appears in learned journals with peer review boards (not popular pseudo-sciences), especially examining spiritual concepts by empirical or statistical methods.

3. *Illustration of Methods.* By way of illustration only and not limitation of the methods the Foundation may use to achieve its purposes, the Foundation may pay for and supervise many varieties of programs of research and of prizes, use various methods of public relations and publications and publicity to increase mankind's comprehension of Humility-in-Theology and its benefits, establish or support organizations whose activities further the purposes of Humility-in-Theology, and educate people of every religion about Humility-in-Theology and its benefits by sponsoring conferences, seminars, lectures and publications, including books and articles, television programs, videos, websites and other media.

B. *Founder's Other Favorite Charities.* From a long life of diligent observation, the Founder considers it more cost-effective and therefore more beneficial to focus on ways to minimize future poverty and sickness than on the popular efforts to relieve existing poverty and sickness. The Foundation's purposes include benefiting humanity by supporting and advancing the following six charities:

1. Supporting education (including education through research and dissemination of the results therefrom) about free competition, entrepreneurship and the enhancement of individual freedom and free markets (especially as described in the writings of Adam

Smith, Friedrich von Hayek, Ludwig von Mises, Milton Friedman and Edwin J. Fuelner, Jr.).

2. Supporting research and publications in genetics (including education through research and dissemination of the results therefrom) with an emphasis on (i) increasing the benefits humanity derives from more geniuses of all attributes worldwide, and (ii) any other benefits derived from the knowledge of genetics.

3. Supporting education and other help in voluntary family planning.

4. Supporting character development research (and dissemination of the results therefrom) and character development programs where character includes, without limitation, ethics, love, honesty, generosity, thanksgiving, forgiving, reliability, entrepreneurship, diligence and thrift.

5. Supporting the publication and dissemination throughout the world of the religious teachings of the Unity School of Christianity of Unity Village, the Association of Unity Churches and of closely similar organizations, provided that major support for such organizations shall continue only so long as the Trustees of the Foundation, as defined in article XIV, determine that such organizations adhere to the concepts of (i) usually pioneering in religion and theology with little restrictive creed, (ii) usually teaching that god may be all of reality and man only a tiny part of god and (iii) generally accentuating the positive ideas and attitudes and avoiding the negative.

6. Supporting the continuation of the Templeton Program of Prizes for Progress in Religion (preferably but not necessarily in the same manner in which such program is carried on at the death of the Founder), especially by awarding prizes to persons who have done something new of a spiritual nature, in any religion, which has resulted in a great increase in man's understanding of god or man's love of god.

C. *Other Charitable Purposes.* The Foundation's purposes include other activities described in Section 501(c)(3) of the Code.

D. The Founder intends for the meaning of the purposes set forth in this article to be construed no differently in the future from their literal meaning on the date of this Charter. The Founder's intention shall limit the Board of Trustees in its deliberations. The Founder believes that to further the Foundation's purposes, particularly Humility-in-Theology, requires continual efforts since the various endeavors to obtain new spiritual information will be never-ending. The Founder further has observed from a lifetime of experience in serving other charitable organizations, and from other personal observations, that the activities of charitable organizations usually drift away from the donor's intent. In order to assist the Board of Trustees, the Foundation management and the members in accomplishing the Foundation's purposes, the Founder has provided in this Charter various requirements designed to alert the Board of Trustees, the Foundation's management and the members to their obligation to conform the Foundation's activities to its purposes.

E. The Board of Trustees shall have the power to use any means that, in the opinion of the Board of Trustees, will help to accomplish these purposes, including contributing to other charitable organizations and contracting with other organizations or independent contractors to conduct, manage or control Foundation programs, or to make or award prizes or grants.

Board of Advisors of the John Templeton Foundation

SPRING 2000

North America

V. Elving Anderson, Ph.D. Professor emeritus of genetics and cell biology; former director of the Dight Laboratories at the University of Minnesota. A diplomate of the American Board of Medical Genetics, his research in human genetics has explored the influence of genetics upon behavior, mental retardation, epilepsy, and breast cancer.

Ian G. Barbour, Ph.D. Professor emeritus in physics and religion at Carleton College in Northfield, Minnesota. In addition to serving as a Gifford Lecturer in 1989-1991, he has written several books addressing the interface of religion and science including *Religion in an Age of Science* and *Ethics in an Age of Technology.*

Herbert Benson, M.D. Associate professor of medicine at the Mind/Body Medical Institute, Harvard Medical School, and president of the Mind/Body Medical Institute at the Beth Israel Deaconess Medical Center. He is the author or co-author of more than 150 scientific publications and six books and the recipient of numerous national and international awards. Dr. Benson is a pioneer in behavioral medicine, mind/body studies and spirituality and healing. His work serves as a bridge between medicine and religion, East and West, mind and body, and belief and science.

Ronald Cole-Turner, M. Div., Ph.D. H. Parker Sharp Associate Professor of Theology and Ethics at Pittsburgh Theological Seminary. He is a member of the Advisory Board of the American Association for the Advancement of Sciences, Program of Dialogue between Science and Religion. He is chair of the United Church of Christ Working Group on Faith, Science, and Technology and Chair of the Task Force on Genetic Engineering for the United Church of Christ. Dr. Cole-Turner has written extensively on the relationship between religion and genetics. He is co-author of the book *Pastoral Genetics: Theology and Care at the Beginning of Life.*

Francis S. Collins, M.D., Ph.D. Physician-geneticist and the director of the National Human Genome Research Institute, NIH. In that role he oversees a thirteen-year project aimed at mapping and sequencing all of the human DNA by the year 2003. He received his Ph.D. in physical chemistry at Yale University and attended medical school at the University of North Carolina. While attending Yale for a fellowship in human genetics, he worked on methods of crossing large stretches of DNA to identify disease genes. Dr. Collins founded a new NIH intramural research program in genome research which has now grown to become one of the premier research units in human genetics in the country. His accomplishments have been recognized by election to the Institute of Medicine and the National Academy of Sciences, and numerous national and international awards.

Lindon J. Eaves, Ph.D. Distinguished professor of human genetics and psychiatry at the Virginia Commonwealth University School of Medicine. He directs the Virginia Institute for Psychiatric and Behavioral Genetics. Dr. Eaves is a priest of the Episcopal church. He has published extensive research involving genetic studies of human behavior and has also published on the interface between religion and science.

Robert A. Emmons, Ph.D. Professor of psychology at the University of California-Davis. He received his doctorate in personality and social ecology from the University of Illinois at Urbana-Champaign. He is the author of more than sixty original publications in peer-reviewed journals or chapters in edited volumes, including his most recent book *The Psychology of Ultimate Concerns:*

Motivation and Spirituality in Personality (Guilford Press), and is a consulting editor for the *Journal of Personality and Social Psychology* and the *International Journal for the Psychology of Religion*. His research focuses on personal goals, spirituality and mental and physical well-being. He has received research funding from the National Institute of Mental Health and the National Institute for Disability Research and Rehabilitation (Department of Education).

Mr. Foster Friess. Chairman of Friess Associates, manager of over $12 billion of equities. A graduate of the University of Wisconsin, he currently serves on the Advisory Council of the Royal Swedish Academy of Sciences of Stockholm, which awards the Nobel Prize for chemistry and physics, and the Executive Committee of the Council for National Policy, which networks leaders in the U.S. who are committed to a strong national defense, traditional values, and the free enterprise system.

Linda K. George, Ph.D. Professor of sociology, psychology and psychiatry at Duke University; associate director of the Duke University Center for the Study of Aging and Human Development and of the Duke University Center for the Study of Religion, Aging and Health. Dr. George is the past president of the Gerontological Society of America and is the author of seven books and nearly two hundred journal articles and chapters. Her research interests include spirituality and health, as well as the effects of stress and social support on health.

Rev. Thomas W. Gillespie, Ph.D. President of Princeton Theological Seminary. Dr. Gillespie is a member of the Presbytery of New Brunswick, the Association of Governing Boards Advisory Council of Presidents and a trustee of the Interdenominational Theological Center in Atlanta, Georgia. He is the author of *The First Theologians: A Study in Early Christian Prophecy.* An alumnus of Princeton Seminary, he earned his doctor of philosophy degree in New Testament Studies from the Claremont Graduate School.

Mr. Kenneth S. Giniger. President of the K. S. Giniger Company, Inc. He has co-published several books with Mr. Templeton that address science and religion. He is chairman of the Layman's National Bible Association.

Mr. Peter Gruber. President of Globalvest Management Company, L.P., a

United-States-based, SEC-registered investment advisor. Mr. Gruber invests globally for private clients and is active in the securities market of Latin America and other emerging markets. Headquartered in St. Thomas, U.S. Virgin Islands, with offices in Rio de Janeiro, Mr. Gruber manages more than $1 billion.

Robert L. Herrmann, Ph.D. Taught medical school biochemistry for twenty-two years. During that time, he developed a keen interest in interrelating science and religion. In 1981 he left medical education to become executive director of the American Scientific Affiliation and a member of the chemistry faculty at Gordon College. While at ASA he met fellow member John Templeton, and they have since cooperated in writing several books, including *The God Who Would Be Known, Is God the Only Reality?* and Sir John's biography. Dr. Herrmann is currently on the staff at Gordon College in Wenham, Massachusetts, where he directs several projects for the John Templeton Foundation.

Mr. Charles E. Johnson. President and chief executive officer of Templeton Worldwide, Inc. and Franklin Institutional Services Corporation. He is senior vice president and director of Franklin Resources, Inc., the parent company of the Templeton organization. Mr. Johnson also serves as a director and/or officer of many of the various Franklin and Templeton mutual funds and subsidiaries. He received an MBA from the Harvard University Graduate School of Business and is a certified public accountant.

Rev. Christopher B. Kaiser, Ph.D. Professor of historical and systematic theology at Western Theological Seminary, Holland, Michigan. Rev. Kaiser has published in the field of historical studies in theology and science and the relation of science, theology, and society.

Harold G. Koenig, M.D. Associate professor of psychiatry and an assistant professor of medicine at Duke University Medical Center. He is the director of the Center for the Study of Religion/Spirituality and Health and the executive editor of the Haworth Pastoral Press mental health and religion book program.

David B. Larson, M.D. Psychiatrist and former senior fellow at the National Institute for Mental Health (NIMH). He is currently president of the

National Institute for Healthcare Research. He has published journal articles and a psychiatric training manual which demonstrate that spirituality and religious practice can benefit physical and mental health and healing.

Martin E. Marty, Ph.D. Senior scholar at Park Ridge Center for the Study of Health, Faith and Ethics in Chicago, Illinois. He is the editor of *Second Opinion,* a journal providing a forum for interface of health, faith and ethics.

Dale Alan Matthews, Ph.D. Associate professor of medicine at Georgetown University School of Medicine, and senior fellow, National Institute for Healthcare Research. He practices and teaches general internal medicine and conducts research on the doctor-patient relationship, patient satisfaction with medical care, the chronic fatigue syndrome, and the psychological and spiritual dimensions of medicine.

Rev. Glenn R. Mosley, M.Sc. Adm., Ph.D. President and CEO of the Association of Unity Churches. His ministry began in 1957, and he has traveled extensively speaking in Unity and non-Unity churches. He frequently serves as a visiting professor for colleges and universities and conducts workshops on interpersonal communications, life and death transitions and integrative healing modalities. He has authored or co-authored a number of books on these topics. He is a trustee of the John Templeton Foundation.

Nancey Murphy, Ph.D. Professor of Christian philosophy at Fuller Theological Seminary, Pasadena, California. Dr. Murphy is on the board of directors of the Center for Theology and the Natural Sciences. Her books include *Theology in the Age of Scientific Reasoning; On the Moral Nature of the Universe: Theology, Cosmology and Ethics* (with G. F. R. Ellis); and *Anglo-American Postmodernity: Philosophical Perspectives on Science, Religion and Ethics.* She is a 1999 recipient of the CTNS Outstanding Books in Theology and Natural Sciences award. Dr. Murphy is an ordained minister in the Church of the Brethren.

Ted Peters, Ph.D. Professor of systematic theology at Pacific Lutheran Theological Seminary and the Graduate Theological Union. He is an active participant at the Center for Theology and the Natural Sciences, where he directs the CTNS-Templeton University Lectures and the CTNS-Templeton Science and Religion Course Program. Dr. Peters was principal investigator for the theological questions raised by the human genome initiative study sponsored by the Human Genome Initiative. He has authored and edited several highly regarded textbooks and research studies in the field of theology, ethics and genetics, including *Playing God? Genetic Determinism and Human Freedom.*

Stephen G. Post, Ph.D. Professor of biomedical ethics at the School of Medicine, Case Western Reserve University. He serves on the National Ethics Advisory Panel of the Alzheimer's Disease and Related Disorders Association and is ethics editor for the journal *Alzheimer Disease and Associated Disorders.* Dr. Post received his doctorate in religious ethics and moral philosophy from the University of Chicago Divinity School. In 1998 he received the annual award for outstanding public service from the Alzheimer's Association. His most recent book is *The Moral Challenge of Alzheimer's Disease.*

V. S. Ramachandran, M.D., Ph.D. Director of the Center for Brain and Cognition, University of California at San Diego. Dr. Ramachandran holds academic positions at both the Salk Institute and the University of California, San Diego, and has published and lectured internationally on the subject of visual neuroscience. He was appointed editor in chief of a four-volume *Encyclopedia of Human Behavior* published by Academic Press.

Mr. Laurance S. Rockefeller. Philanthropist, business executive and conservationist. He has held various chairs and trustee appointments for a wide number of national, academic and humanitarian organizations. Mr. Rockefeller has been the recipient of many awards and medals for his conservation work and philanthropic interests, including the Congressional Gold Medal in 1991.

Robert J. Russell, Ph.D. Founder and director of the Center for Theology and the Natural Sciences (CTNS) and professor of theology and science in residence at The Graduate Theological Union in Berkeley, California. He received his Ph.D. in physics from the University of California at Santa Cruz, and his specialized interests include inflationary and quantum cosmology and philosophical foundations of quantum mechanics. Dr. Russell has co-edited five books on theology and science as a result of ongoing collaborative research between CTNS and the Vatican Observatory. He is a former judge for the Templeton Prize for Progress in Religion and works closely with the CTNS Science and Religion Course Program and Science and the Spiritual Quest.

Allan Sandage, Ph.D. Graduate of the University of Illinois. He received his Ph.D. in astronomy from the California Institute of Technology. Dr. Sandage began his career at Mount Wilson Observatory when he was chosen by Edgar Hubble to work as his personal assistant. He has achieved recognition for his work in stellar evolution, the composition of galaxies and observational high-energy astrophysics. He is best known for his pathfinding work in observational cosmology, measuring the rate of expansion and the age of the universe. He is a recipient of numerous awards for his work, including the Presidential Medal of Science and the American Astronomical Society's Russell Prize. Dr. Sandage was visiting professor at John Hopkins University for 1986-1987 in the department of physics and astronomy and senior visiting fellow at the Space Telescope Science Institute.

Rev. Lawrence E. Sullivan, Ph.D. Director of the Harvard University Center for the Study of World Religions, professor of religion, past president of the American Academy of Religions and deputy secretary-general of the International Association for the History of Religions. He has received numerous awards, including a 1996-1997 Henry Luce fellowship. He is the author of many articles and editor of several books, and he received the American Council of Learned Societies Book Award for Best First Book and the Award for Best Book in Philosophy and Religion given by the Association of American Publishers for *Icanchu's Drum: An Orientation to Meaning in South American Religions.*

Charles H. Townes, Ph.D. Professor in the Graduate School at the University of California, Berkeley and a Nobel Prize recipient in physics. He has published articles with regard to science and theology. Dr. Townes's research was primarily responsible for the development of the laser.

Lynn G. Underwood, Ph.D. Vice President of the Fetzer Institute where she develops collaborative research projects with other organizations and does program planning, review, and evaluation. She spent ten years in the field of cancer epidemiology doing research into pathogenesis, prevention, and early detection. Her current research interests include the role of various dimensions of religiousness and spirituality in living with disability.

Howard J. Van Till, Ph.D. Professor and chairman of the department of physics at Calvin College, Grand Rapids, Michigan. He is a member of the American Astronomical Society and the American Scientific Affiliation. He has written books and articles addressing creation and cosmology from a Christian perspective.

Everett L. Worthington, Jr., Ph.D. Professor of psychology at Virginia Commonwealth University. In 1986 he published an extensive review of research on religion in counseling and recently provided a ten-year update to the review, which was published in *Psychological Bulletin*. Dr. Worthington has published more than seventy-five scientific articles in peer-reviewed journals on the role of spirituality in health and healthcare.

Eurasia/Australia

John D. Barrow, Ph.D. Professor of mathematical sciences and director of the Millennium Mathematics Project in the department of applied mathematical and theoretical physics at the University of Cambridge and a fellow of Clare Hall College. He is a leading researcher in cosmology and a well-known communicator of science who has written three hundred papers and twelve books, including *Theories of Everything, Pi in the Sky, The Left Hand of Creation, The Origin of the Universe, The Anthropic Cosmological Principle, The World Within the World, Between Inner Space and Outer Space* and *The Artful Universe*. He has received the Locker Award for Astronomy and received the 1999 Kelvin Medal.

R. J. Berry, D. Sc. Professor of genetics at University College, London. He was previously the chairman of several ecological organizations and Research Scientists' Christian Fellowship (now Christians in Science). He is currently chairman of the Environmental Issues Network of CCBI. Professor Berry has lectured and published extensively with regard to the preservation of the environment.

Paul C. Davies, Ph.D. Visiting professor at Imperial College, London, and honorary professor at the University of Queensland. Dr. Davies received his doctorate from University College, London, and was appointed professor of theoretical physics at the University of Newcastle upon Tyne. He had served as professor of mathematical physics, and later natural philosophy, at the University of Adelaide. Based in South Australia, Dr. Davies runs a science, media and publishing consultancy called Orion Productions. He has published over one hundred research papers in specialist journals in the fields of cosmology, gravitation, and quantum field theory with particular emphasis on black holes and the origin of the universe. Dr. Davies was the 1995 recipient of the Templeton Prize for Progress in Religion.

George F. R. Ellis, Ph.D. Visiting lecturer and professor in cosmology, physics and astronomy across the globe, including South Africa, England, Germany, Canada, Italy and the United States. He received his Ph.D. in applied maths and theoretical physics from the St. John's College at Cambridge, is a fellow of the Royal Society of South Africa, and was president of the International Society of Relativity and Gravitation. Dr. Ellis is co-author of *On the Moral Nature of the Universe: Theology, Cosmology and Ethics* (Theology and the Sciences) with fellow foundation advisor Nancey Murphy, and he has collaborated with Stephen Hawking on a number of publications, including *The Large Scale Structure of Space Time.*

Bruno Guiderdoni, Ph.D. Astrophysicist at the French National Center for Scientific Research (CNRS). His research field at the Paris Institute of Astrophysics is mainly related to galaxy formation. Since 1993, he has been in charge of the weekly TV show "Knowing Islam" of the State Channel France 2. In his papers and lectures, he attempts to present the intellectual and spiritual aspects of Islam, reflect upon the relation between science and the Islamic tradition, and promote an interreligious dialogue.

Peter E. Hodgson, Ph.D. Head of nuclear physics theoretical group, Nuclear Physics Laboratory, Oxford, and senior research fellow at Corpus Christi College. He has published widely on the subject of the future effection of nuclear energy applications as well as in the area of Christianity and science.

Malcolm Jeeves, Ph.D. Research professor of psychology, University of St. Andrews. He is president of The Royal Society of Edinburgh and was made Commander of the Order of the British Empire in the Queen's National New

Year's Honours in 1992 for his services to science and to psychology in Britain. He established the department of psychology at St. Andrews, and his research interests center around cognitive psychology and neuropsychology.

Stephen C. Orchard, M.A., Ph.D. Director of the Christian Education Movement and a minister of the United Reform Church. He is chairman of the British Foreign School Society and an honorary professor of the education faculty of Brunel University. He is secretary of the Religious Education Council of England and Wales. He was formerly associate general secretary of the British Council of Churches. He serves in various honorary capacities in the United Reformed Church, and his hymns and prayers appear in collections in the United Kingdom and the U.S.

Rev. Arthur R. Peacock, Ph.D. Warden emeritus of the Society of Ordained Scientists and honorable chaplain of Christ Church Cathedral, Oxford. He is also the director of the Ian Ramsey Centre, Oxford University. He has been the recipient of the Le Compte DuNuoy Prize, and his primary discipline is the physical chemistry of biological systems. A 1993 Gifford Lecturer, his religion and science writings include his recent book *Theology for a Science Age.*

Jean Staune, Ph.D. Assistant professor in philosophy of science in the MBA section of HEC (Paris). He has several degrees from French universities and Grandes Ecoles in philosophy of science, human paleontology, computer science, mathematics, economy and management. Dr. Staune is the founder and general secretary of the Interdisciplinary University of Paris (IUP), which has organized some of the most important meetings in science and religion in Europe. He is the director of a series of books, *Le Temps des Sciences at Editions Fayard* (Hachette Group). His current research concerns the meeting point between contemporary discoveries in physics, astronomy, mathematics, biology, neurology and the probability of the existence of God.

Keith Ward, Ph.D. Regius professor of divinity at the University of Oxford and formerly professor of history and philosophy of religion at King's College, London University. He is one of the country's foremost writers on comparative religion and Christian issues. A Gifford lecturer, his most recent book, *Defending the Soul,* is an affirmation of human divinity and value.

Trustees and Members
of the John Templeton Foundation

SPRING 2000

Trustees
Dr. John D. Barrow
Mrs. Ann T. Cameron
Dr. Paul Davies
Mrs. Heather E. Dill
Dr. Robert L. Herrmann
Rev. Bryant Kirkland
Rev. Glenn R. Mosely
Dr. David G. Myers
Mr. William E. Simon
Sir John M. Templeton
Dr. John M. Templeton, Jr.
Dr. Anne D. Zimmerman

Members
Mr. Baba Amte
Prof. Ian Barbour
Prof. Charles Birch
Rev. Canon Michael Bourdeaux
Mrs. Wendy Brooks
Mrs. Amy Van Hoose Butler

Mrs. Ann T. Cameron
Mr. Douglas Cameron
Mr. Robert Handly Cameron
Mrs. Leigh Cameron
Miss Jennifer Cameron
Dr. Paul Davies
Mrs. Heather E. Dill
Mr. Jeffrey Dill
Mr. Charles R. Fillmore
Mrs. Connie Fillmore Bazzy
Dr. Edwin J. Feulner
Mrs. Wilhelmina Griffiths
Dr. Kyung-Chik Han
Dr. Robert L. Herrmann
Prof. Colin Humphreys
Prof. Stanley Jaki
Mrs. Elizabeth Kernan
Mr. Josh Kernan
Rev. Bryant Kirkland
Mrs. Avery Lloyd
Mr. David W. Lloyd

Recipients, Judges, Former Judges and Presiding Officers of The Templeton Prize for Progress in Religion

RECIPIENTS

1973 Mother Teresa of Calcutta, who was founder of the Missionaries of Charity. She saw Christ in "the poorest of the poor" in what has become a worldwide ministry to the dying.

1974 Brother Roger, founder and prior of the Taizé Community in France. Taizé Communes have appeared all over the world, bridging many denominations and languages.

1975 Sir Sarvepalli Radhakrishnan, who was president of India and Oxford professor of Eastern religions and ethics. He is a strong proponent of religious idealism as the most hopeful political instrument for peace.

1976 His Excellency Leon Joseph Cardinal Suenens, who was Archbishop of Malines-Brussels. He was a pioneer of the charismatic renewal and a strong proponent of Christian unity.

1977 Chiara Lubich, founder of the Focolare Movement, Italy, which has become a worldwide network of over a million people in communes and private homes engaged in spiritual renewal and ecumenism.

1978   Professor Thomas F. Torrance, who was moderator of the Church of Scotland. He is a leader in the new understanding of the convergence of theology and science.

1979   Reverend Nikkyo Niwano, founder of Rishho Kosei-Kai and World Conference on Religion and Peace, Japan. He is a Buddhist world leader in efforts toward peace and understanding among religious groups.

1980   Professor Ralph Wendell Burhoe, founder and former editor of *Zygon* journal, Chicago, Illinois, U.S. He is a leading advocate of an intellectually credible synthesis of the religious and scientific traditions.

1981   Dame Cicely Saunders, originator of the modern hospice movement, England. She is a pioneer in the care of the terminally ill by emphasizing spiritual growth and modern methods of pain management.

1982   The Reverend Dr. Billy Graham, founder of the Billy Graham Evangelistic Association, U.S.A. He has preached the Christian gospel in over fifty countries, brought diverse denominations together and promoted respect for all peoples.

1983   Mr. Aleksandr Solzhenitsyn, Russia. He is a historical writer and novelist who has been an outspoken critic of totalitarianism and a strong proponent of spiritual awakening in the democracies as well.

1984   The Reverend Michael Bourdeaux, founder of Keston College, England, a research center for the study of religion in communist countries. He has been a fearless supporter of Christians in Russia.

1985   Sir Alister Hardy, who was founder of the Sir Alister Hardy Research Centre at Oxford, England. An outstanding biologist, he also had a deep interest in man's spiritual nature. His work has demonstrated widespread religious experience in the British Isles.

1986   Reverend Dr. James McCord, who was chancellor of the Center of Theological Inquiry, Princeton, New Jersey, U.S. He was a leader in theological education as president of Princeton Theological Seminary.

1987   Reverend Professor Stanley L. Jaki, O.S.B., professor of astrophysics at Seton Hall University, New York, U.S. He has provided a reinterpretation of the history of science which provides a context for renewed belief in god in a scientific age.

1988   Dr. Inamullah Khan, who was secretary-general, World Muslim Congress, Karachi, Pakistan, and a proponent of peace within and between the world's religions.

1989   The Very Reverend Lord MacLeod, of the Iona Community, Scotland. He is a leader for spiritual renewal in the Church of Scotland.

Jointly with

Professor Carl Friedrich von Weizacker of Starnberg, West Germany. A physicist and philosopher, he is a strong voice for dialogue between science and theology.

1990   Baba Amte, of the Anandwan community, India. He is a learned Hindu scholar and philanthropist who relieved the poverty of millions in rural India.

Jointly with

Professor Charles Birch, a biologist, Sydney, Australia. He is a molecular biologist and strong proponent of process theology and environmental stewardship.

1991   The Right Honourable Lord Jakobovits, former chief rabbi of Great Britain and the Commonwealth. He is a leader in Jewish concern for medicine and especially medical ethics.

1992   The Reverend Dr. Kyung-Chik Han, a Presbyterian pastor, Seoul, Korea. He was a pioneer in helping the Presbyterian church to become in only thirty years the largest Presbyterian congregation in Korea.

1993   Mr. Charles W. Colson, founder of Prison Fellowship, Washington, D.C., U.S. He is a strong Christian force for change in the American prison system.

1994   Mr. Michael Novak, philosopher and theologian, Washington, D.C., U.S. He is a powerful voice for reemphasis of our rich religious and philosophical traditions.

1995   Professor Paul Davies, scientist, Adelaide, South Australia. He is a leading authority in expounding the idea of purpose in the universe and author of more than twenty books.

1996   Dr. William R. Bright, evangelist, Orlando, Florida, U.S. He leads and originated the Campus Crusade for Christ International, which has helped revitalize a love for god to millions of students and laypeople.

1997   Sri Pandurang Shastri Athavale, founder of the Swadhyaya Movement, Bombay, India. Motivated by a deep commitment to the service of god, Mr. Athavale has enabled several million Indian villagers to experience a better way of life through a spiritual revolution.

1998   Sir Sigmund Sternberg, layman, London. He has pioneered and proved inter-religious dialogue as a new force for reconciliation and the understanding of god.

1999   Professor Ian Barbour has been one of the world pioneers in the integration of science and religion. His books and articles are helping to expand the field of theology not only for Christians but also for other faiths.

2000   Professor Freeman J. Dyson is professor of physics at the Institute for Advanced Study, Princeton, N.J. He has been widely published for his work in physics and ethics in science with regard to arms control.

Judges

Dr. M. A. Zaki Badawi, London, United Kingdom

Dr. Paul Davies, Adelaide, South Australia

Mr. Rich DeVos, Michigan, U.S.

Mr. Robert Galvin, Illinois, U.S.

Professor Mendi Golshani, Tehran, Iran

Dr. Robert L. Herrmann, Massachusetts, U.S.

Dr. Ravi Ravindra, Halifax, Canada

Mrs. Helen Robson Walton, Arkansas, U.S.

Lord Weidenfeld, London, United Kingdom

Former Judges

The Duchess of Abercorn, Northern Ireland

The Duke of Abercorn, Northern Ireland

His All Holiness Ecumenical Patriarch Bartholomew, Turkey

His Royal Highness Prince Albert of Belgium

Mr. Norman E. Alexander, U.S.

The Honorable Walter H. Annenberg, U.S.

Mr. K. Shankar Bajpai, India

Justice P. N. Bhagwatti, India

Dr. James Billington, U.S.

The Reverend Dr. Eugene Carson Blake, U.S.

The Most Reverend Stuart Blanch, United Kingdom

The Viscount Brentford, England

Mr. George Bush, Former President of the United States

The Right Reverend and Right Honourable Lord Coggan,
   United Kingdom

Professor Suniti Kumar Chatterji, Bengal

Mrs. Winifred Crothers, Nassau, The Bahamas

The Dalai Lama, Tibet

Senator John C. Danforth, U.S.

His All Holiness Demetrois I., Turkey

Mr. Asakazu Echigo, Japan

Her Majesty Fabiola, Belgium

Mr. Charles R. Fillmore, U.S.

Mr. Gerald Ford, Former President of the United States
Mr. James Dillet Freeman, U.S.
Mr. George Gallup, Jr., U.S.
Mr. J. Peter Grace, U.S.
The Right Honourable Lord Griffiths, England
The Most Reverend John Habgood, England
Mr. Yasuf A. Haroon, Pakistan
Senator Orrin G. Hatch, U.S.
Senator Mark O. Hatfield, U.S.
The Right Honourable Lord Howe, England
Dr. Inamullah Khan, Pakistan
Sir Muhammad Zafrulla Khan, The Netherlands
The Right Honourable Lord Kingdown, England
Dr. Margaretha Klompe, The Netherlands
Mr. Philip M. Klutznick, U.S.
Dr. Harry G. Kuch, U.S.
Dr. Carl M. Kuttler, Jr., U.S.
Sir Bernard Lovell, England
Her Royal Highness the Grand Duchess Josephine of Luxembourg
Dr. David McCaughey, Australia
The Reverend Dr. James I. McCord, U.S.
The Most Reverend Mark McGrath, Panama
Sir Alan Macotta, England
The Reverend David Mainse, Canada
The Right Reverend Sir Michael Mann, United Kingdom
The Honourable Sir Clement Maynard, The Bahamas
The Right Honourable Lord Menuhin, England
Dr. Glenn R. Mosley, U.S.
Reverend Nichiko Niwano, Japan
Reverend Nikkyo Niwano, Japan
Major General The Duke of Norfolk, K.G., England
The Lord Abbot Kosho Ohtani, Japan
The Reverend Dr. Stephen Orchard, Derby, United Kingdom
Mr. Nani A. Palkhivala, India

The Honourable Apasaheb Balasaheb Pant, India
Dr. Arthur R. Peacocke, England
The Reverend Dr. Norman Vincent Peale, U.S.
The Right Honourable Sir Lynden Pindling, The Bahamas
Her Serene Highness Princess Poon Pismai Diskul, Thailand
Mr. Edward S. Rogers, Canada
Mr. Edmund Leopold de Rothschild, England
The Reverend Dr. Robert J. Russell, U.S.
Mrs. Anwar el Sadat, Egypt
Mr. William E. Simon, U.S.
Dr. Nagendra Singh, The Netherlands
Sir Sigmund Sternberg, England
The Right Reverend John V. Taylor, England
Baroness Thatcher, England
The Right Honourable The Lord Thurlow, England
The Honourable Leo Tindemans, Belgium
The Right Honourable The Viscount Tonypandy, P.C., England
His Royal Highness, the Prince of Wales
The Right Honourable Lord Wigoder, Q.C., England
The Right Reverend Sir Robin Woods, England
Dr. Anne D. Zimmerman, U.S.

Chairpersons

1973	His Royal Highness The Duke of Edinburgh
1974	The Right Honourable The Earl of March
1975	The Right Reverend and Right Honourable Lord Coggan
1976	The Right Honourable Margaret Thatcher, P.C., M.P.
1977	Johannes Cardinal Willebrands
1978	The Reverend Dr. James I. McCord
1979	The Honourable Leo Tindemans
1980	Lady Marguerite Pindling
1981	The Right Honourable Lord Rees-Mogg
1982	The Right Honourable Lord Howe, P.C., M.P.
1983	The Right Honourable Lord Pritchard

1984	The Right Honourable Sir Edward duCann, K.B.E.
1985	His Grace, The Duke of Norfolk, K.G.
1986	The Right Honourable Viscount Tonypandy, P.C.
1987	Sir Anthony Kenny
1988	—
1989	Mr. Takeo Fukuda
1990	The Duke of Abercorn
1991	(Toronto) The Right Honourable Jeanne Suavé
1991	(Vancouver) The Honourable David Lam
1992	Dr. Otto von Habsburg
1993	Joseph Cardinal Bernardin
1994	The Reverend Dr. Colin Morris
1995	The Right Honourable Viscount Tonypandy, P.C.
1996	Edward Cardinal Cassidy
1997	The Reverend Jonathan Goodall
1998	Mr. Maurice Strong
1999	Reverend Dr. Alexei Bodrov
2000	The Honorable James H. Billington

Catalog of Templeton Foundation Press

SPIRITUALITY AND INSPIRATION

Worldwide Worship
Prayers, Songs, and Poetry
Edited by John Marks Templeton
A unique celebration of worship found in many religious traditions, these selections have been chosen not only for their individual aesthetic beauty but also to assist us in learning various lessons of life. 1-890151-35-1, $24.95 hbd

Pure Unlimited Love
Sir John Templeton
Is agape love an action, a universal energy, or a creative force? And can its expression ever be realized, or is it simply a divine attribute? These and other questions are addressed in an inspirational and practical style in this thoughtful essay from Sir John Templeton. 1-890151-41-6, $6.95 pbk

Agape Love
A Tradition Found in Eight World Religions
Sir John Templeton
A beautiful gift book for inspiration and guidance. The tradition of agape, or unconditional love, is not exclusive to any one religion.
1-890151-29-7, $12.95 hbd

Spiritual Investments
Wall Street Wisdom from the Career of Sir John Templeton
Gary Moore
Gathered here are seventeen sound investment principles that will help people make sensible choices for financial security. What is surprising, however, is how applicable these principles are to life. 1-890151-18-1, $12.95 hbd

Worldwide Laws of Life
200 Eternal Spiritual Principles
Edited by John Marks Templeton
Wisdom drawn from major sacred scriptures of the world and various schools of philosopical thought, as well as from scientists, artists, historians, and others. Thoughtfully arranged in a format that can be used as a resource for discussion groups.0-890151-15-7, $14.95 pbk; 0-8264-1018-9, $24.95 hbd

Golden Nuggets
Sir John Templeton
Practical and uplifting advice, based on a lifetime of experience, is gathered in an attractive package for one's personal use or as a perfect gift.
1-890151-04-1, $12.95 hbd

SCIENCE AND RELIGION

God for the 21st Century
Edited by Russell Stannard
Just as modern science has revolutionized our understanding of the natural world, so can it expand our understanding of the divine. In topics ranging from astronomy to cosmology, from genetic engineering to artificial intelligence, fifty key figures discuss the interrelationship between science and religion. 1-890151-39-4, $12.95 pbk. 1-890151-36-X, $19.95 hbd

Many Worlds
The New Universe, Extraterrestrial Life, and the Theological Implications
Edited by Steven J. Dick
Discussing the possibility of a cosmic evolutionary process, a renowned group of scientists ponder whether our existence is part of a divine scheme ingenuously designed to support life.
1-890151-42-4; $14.95 pbk; 1-890151-37-8, $22.95 hbd

God, Science, and Humility
Ten Scientists Consider Humility Theology
Edited by Robert L. Herrmann
Ten scientists consider humility theology—a humble approach to our truth seeking about God—in a book that will significantly help the reader in the search for greater understanding of the relationship between science and religion. 1-890151-34-3, $19.95 pbk

The Mind of the Universe
Understanding Science and Religion
Mariano Artigas
Written by a philosopher and physicist, *The Mind of the Universe* provides a suitable basis for a perspective that includes purpose and religious values. Artigas offers a comprehensive overview of this exciting new field of study. 1-890151-32-7, $22.95 hbd

The Cosmic Dance
Science Discovers the Mysterious Harmony of the Universe
Giuseppe Del Re
Focusing on a new worldview emerging from science, *The Cosmic Dance* evaluates the harmony between interdependent systems that behave as one. Grounded in universal principles of science, a pattern of great spiritual potential emerges that suggests God's divine intentions.
1-890151-25-4, $24.95 hbd

The God Who Would Be Known
Revelations of the Divine in Contemporary Science
John Marks Templeton and Robert L. Herrmann
This book highlights the understanding, meaning and purpose in the universe as well as learning about God through scientific studies.
1-890151-20-3, $14.95 pbk

Spiritual Evolution
Scientists Discuss Their Beliefs
Edited by John Marks Templeton and Kenneth Seeman Giniger
Charles Birch, S. Jocelyn Bell Burnell, Larry Dossey, Owen Gingerich, Peter E. Hodgson, Stanley L. Jaki, Arthur Peacocke, John Polkinghorne, Russell Stannard, and Carl Friedrich von Weizsacker offer accounts of their spirituality and scientific inquiry. 1-890151-16-5, $18.95 hbd

How Large Is God?
The Voices of Scientists and Theologians
Edited by John Marks Templeton
This challenging book furthers the theological and philosophical implications of accelerating scientific discoveries of our times.
1-890151-01-7, $22.95 hbd

Evidence of Purpose
Scientists Discover the Creator
Edited by John Marks Templeton
A thought-provoking collection of essays by respected scientists who explore new developments in their fields and the consequent theological implications. 0-8264-06491-1, $24.50 hbd

Is God the Only Reality?
Science Points to a Deeper Meaning of the Universe
John Marks Templeton and Robert L. Herrmann
Examining discoveries in fields such as particle physics and molecular biology, the authors address the great paradox of science that the more we learn, the more mysterious the universe becomes.
0-8264-0650-5; $22.95 hbd

BUSINESS AND FREEDOM

Sir John Templeton
From Wall Street to Humility Theology
Robert L. Herrmann
An inspirational biography of Sir John Templeton and his own search for meaning and spiritual expression. Dedicated to promoting spiritual progress, Sir John believes that the limitless potential of religion needs to be unlocked. 1-890151-00-9, $19.95 hbd; 1-890151-27-0, $12.95 pbk

Looking Forward
The Next Forty Years
Edited by John Marks Templeton
Inspiring essays from world leaders indicating positive appraisal of the next forty years. It includes essays by Owen Gingerich, Theodore M. Hesburgh, David Brown, Denton A. Cooley, Orrin G. Hatch, Robert L. Herrmann, Armand M. Nicholi, Jr., Ruth Stafford Peale, Ghillean T. Prance and John M. Templeton. 1-890151-05-X, $14.95 pbk

Is Progress Speeding Up?
Our Multiplying Multitudes of Blessings
John Marks Templeton
The statistics, charts, and photographs that illustrate this book help to provide a reassuring and uplifting view of the state of the world and where it is going. 1-890151-02-5, $19.95 hbd

Extraordinary Popular Delusions and the Madness of Crowds
Charles Mackay
This classic rings as true today as it did when first published in 1841. Mackay debunks scams, grand-scale madness, and deception through common sense and crowd psychology. 1-890151-40-8, $19.95 pbk

CHARACTER DEVELOPMENT

Colleges That Encourage Character Development
A Resource for Parents, Students, and Educators
The Templeton Guide
Edited by the John Templeton Foundation
This comprehensive guidebook offers parents and students the opportunity to evaluate colleges that promote character education.
1-890151-28-9, $16.95 pbk

LAWS OF LIFE SYMPOSIA SERIES

The Science of Optimism and Hope
Research Essays in Honor of Martin E. P. Seligman
Edited by Jane E. Gillham
Examines the resilient nature of the human spirit when optimism and hope are restored. Eminent psychologists discuss the dynamic relationship between happiness and greater spiritual awareness. 1-890151-26-2, $19.95 pbk
1-890151-24-6, $29.95 hbd

Understanding Wisdom
Sources, Science, and Society
Edited by Warren S. Brown
Evidence of wisdom can be seen in both perception and performance, in sacred scriptures and in brain images. This volume sheds light on the age-old questions: What is wisdom? and Where does it come from? 1-890151-30-0, $19.95 pbk; 1-890151-31-9, $29.95 hbd

Dimensions of Forgiveness
Psychological Research and Theological Perspectives
Edited by Everett L. Worthington, Jr.
This new field of study reveals the powerful benefits to the forgiveness process and provides a comprehensive overview of how and why forgiveness works. 1-890151-22-X, $14.95 pbk; 1-890151-21-1, $22.95 hbd

For a complete listing of titles available visit our web site
www.templetonpress.org
To order books call 800-621-2736

TEMPLETON FOUNDATION PRESS
Five Radnor Corporate Center
Suite 120
100 Matsonford Road
Radnor, Pennsylvania 19087

Science and Religion Organizations

American Scientific Affiliation
55 Market Street
Box 668
Ipswich, MA 01938-0668
Phone: 978-356-5656
Fax: 978-356-4375

Australasian Association for
  Process Thought
P.O. Box 23
Newtown NSW 2042
Australia
Phone: 61-2-9517-2938

Boston University Ph.D. Program
  in Science and Religion
745 Commonwealth Avenue
Boston, MA 02215
Phone: 617-353-6788
Fax: 617-353-3062

Canadian Scientific
  Christian Affiliation
P.O. Box 40086
75 King Street S
Waterloo ON N2J 4V1

Center for Bioethics and Human
  Dignity
2065 Half Day Road
Bannockburn, IL 60015
Phone: 847-317-8180
Fax: 847-317-8153

Center for Business, Religion and
  Public Life
Pittsburgh Theological Seminary
616 North Highland Avenue
Pittsburgh, PA 15206-2596
Phone: 412-362-5610 x2195
Phone: 412-363-3260

Center for Process Studies
1325 N. College Avenue
Claremont, CA 91711-3154
Phone: 909-621-5330
Fax: 909-621-2760

Center for the Studies of Values
  in Public Life
Harvard Divinity School
56 Francis Avenue
Cambridge, MA 02138
Phone: 617-253-7891

Center for the Study of Religion,
    Spirituality, and Health
Duke University Medical Center
DUMC-3400
Durham, NC 27710
Phone: 919-383-6962

Center for Theology and the
    Natural Sciences
2400 Ridge Road
Berkeley, CA 94709-1212
Phone: 510-848-8152
Fax: 510-848-2535

Center of Theological Inquiry
50 Stockton Street
Princeton, NJ 08540
Phone: 609-683-4797
Fax: 609-683-4030

Centre for Science & Religion
Hopewell House
173 Woodhouse Lane
University of Leeds
Leeds LS2 9JT
United Kingdom
Phone: 44 (0) 113-233 6746
Fax: 44 (0) 113-233 3654

Christians in Science
88 Sylvandale
Welywyn Garden City AL7 2HT
United Kingdom
Phone: 44 (0) 1707-390448

Christians in Science Education
5 Longcrofte Road
Edgeware HA8 6RR
United Kingdom
Phone: 44 (0) 1819-525-349

Cosmos and Creation
Loyola College
4501 N. Charles Street
Baltimore, MD 21210-2699
Phone: 410-617-5617
Fax: 410-617-2803

Council for a Parliament of the
    World's Religions
P.O. Box 1630
Chicago, IL 60690-1630
Phone: 312-629-2990
Fax: 312-629-3552

Counterbalance Foundation
2030 Dexter Avenue N.
Suite B296
Seattle, WA 98109
Phone: 206-718-7300
Fax: 206-718-7300

Ecumenical Roundtable
Pittsburgh Theological
    Seminary
616 N. Highland Avenue
Pittsburgh, PA 15206
Phone: 412-441-3304

ESSSAT
Hogserods prastgard
S-240 33
Loberod
Sweden
Phone: 46 413 30398
Fax: 46 413 30398

Fetzer Institute
9292 West KL Avenue
Kalamazoo, MI 49009-9398
Phone: 616-375-2000

Georgetown Center for the
  Study of Science and Religion
Department of Theology
Georgetown University
Washington, DC 20057-1135
Phone: 202-687-6119

Ian Ramsey Centre
Faculty of Theology of Oxford
41 Giles Street
Oxford, OX1 3LW
United Kingdom
Phone: 44 (0) 1865-270-792

Institute for the Study of
  Christianity in an Age of
  Science and Technology
5 Savoy Avenue
Killara 2071
Australia
Phone: 61 2 9498 2710

Institute for Ultimate Reality
  and Meaning
St. Paul's College
70 Dysart Road
Winnipeg MB R3T 2M6
Canada
Phone: 204-474-7186
Fax: 204-474-7613

Institute for Noetic Sciences
475 Gate Five Road, Suite 300
Sausalito, CA 06798
Phone: 415-331-5650
Fax: 415-331-5673

Institute on Religion in an Age
  of Science
29 Hollow Road
Woodbury, CT 06798
Phone: 203-557-4540
Fax: 203-557-4581

International Institute of Islamic
  Thought
1145 Herndon Parkway
Suite 500
Herndon, VA 20170
Phone: 703-471-1133
Fax: 703-471-3922

John Templeton Foundation
Five Radnor Corporate Center
Suite 100
100 Matsonford Road
Radnor, PA 19087
Phone: 610-687-8942
Fax: 610-687-8961

Karl-Heim-Gesellschaft
Unter den Eichen 13
Marburg
D-35041 Germany
Phone: 49-0-64-21-9-80-14
Fax: 49-0-64-21-9-80-16

National Institute for Healthcare
  Research (NIHR)
6110 Executive Boulevard
Suite 908
Rockville, MD 20852
Phone: 301-984-7162
Fax: 301-984-8143

New England Center for Faith
  and Science Exchange
Boston Theological Institute
210 Herrick Road
Newton Centre, MA 02459
Phone: 617-527-4880
Fax: 617-527-1073

Pascal Centre
Redeemer College
777 Garner Road East
Ancaster ON L9K 1J4
Canada
Phone: 905-648-2139
Fax: 905-648-2134

Paul Tillich Society
Department of Religious Studies
Santa Clara University
Santa Clara, CA 95053

Philadelphia Center for Religion
  and Science
3741 Walnut Street, #429
Philadelphia, PA 19104
Phone: 610-486-1176

Pontifical Catholic University
  of Sao Paulo
R. Monte Alegra, 984
Sao Paulo SP 05014
Brazil
Phone: 55-11-3670-8529
Fax: 55-11-3670-8529

Presbyterian Association
  on Science
917 Forest Avenue
Pittsburgh, PA 15202-1117
Phone: 202-326-7044

Program of Dialogue on Science,
  Ethics and Religion (AAAS)
1200 New York Avenue, NW
Washington, DC 20005
Phone: 202-326-6400

Science and Religion Forum
St. Albans Vicarage
Mercer Avenue
Coventry, CV2 4PQ
United Kingdom
Phone: 44 (24) 7645 2493

Science and Spirit Resources
P.O. Box 1145
171-B Rumford Street
Concord, NH 03302-1145
Phone: 603-226-3328
Fax: 603-229-0953

Scientific and Medical Network
Gibliston Mill
Colinsburgh, Leven
Fife KY9 1JS
United Kingdom
Phone: 44(0) 1333-340492
Fax: 44(0) 1333-340491

Society of Ordained Scientists
Stamford Cottage
47 Old Road
Mottram, Hyde
Cheshire SK14 6LW
United Kingdom
Phone: 44 (0) 1457-763-104

South African Science and
  Religion Forum
University of Natal, Physics
  Department
Durban, Dalbridge
4014 South Africa
Fax: 27-31-261-6550

Tapestry: The Institute for
  Philosophy, Religion, and Life
  Studies
100 N. 6th Street, Suite 702
Waco, TX 76701
Phone: 254-752-5590

Universite Interdisciplinaire
  de Paris
29, rue Viala
Paris 75015 France
Phone: 33 (0) 1-45-78-85-52
Fax: 33 (0) 1-45-78-85-09

Zygon Center for Science and
  Religion (formerly CCRS)
1100 East 55th Street
Chicago, Illinois 60615-5199
Phone: 312-753-0670